THE SECRET ADAM

A Study of Naṣoraean Gnosis

THE SECRET ADAM

A Study of Naṣoraean Gnosis

BY

E. S. DROWER, Hon. D.Litt.

HON. FELLOW OF THE
SCHOOL OF ORIENTAL AND AFRICAN STUDIES
UNIVERSITY OF LONDON

WIPF & STOCK · Eugene, Oregon

Wipf and Stock Publishers
199 W 8th Ave, Suite 3
Eugene, OR 97401

The Secret Adam
A Study of Nasoraean Gnosis
By Drower, E. S.

ISBN 13: 978-1-5326-9763-0
Publication date 3/31/2020
Previously published by Oxford University Press, 1960

CONTENTS

ABBREVIATIONS *page* vii

INTRODUCTION ix

I. IN THE BEGINNING 1

II. THE FATHER AND MOTHER: THE ALPHABET 12

III. ADAM KASIA, THE SECRET OR HIDDEN ADAM 21

IV. ADAM AND HIS SONS 34

V. MŠUNIA KUŠṬA: THE WORLD OF IDEAL COUNTERPARTS 39

VI. THE SOUL 47

VII. PERSONIFIED EMANATIONS AND 'UTHRAS 56

VIII. MYSTERIES AND THE GREAT MYSTERY 66

IX. THE LANGUAGE AND IDIOM OF NAṢIRUTHA 81

X. THE BAPTIZERS AND THE SECRET ADAM 88

EPILOGUE 107

APPENDIX 111

MANDAEAN SOURCES 114

INDEX 117

ABBREVIATIONS

A-N	Ante-Nicene.
ARR	Alma Rišaia Rba, Bodleian Library MS. *DC* 41.
ARZ	Alma Rišaia Zuṭa, Bodleian Library MS. *DC* 48.
ATŠ	*Alf Trisar Šuialia*, trans. E. S. Drower. (Published 1960 by the Institut für Orientforschung, Deutsche Akademie der Wissenschaften, Berlin, under the title *1012 Questions*.)
CP	*The Canonical Prayerbook of the Mandaeans*: Text, notes, and translation by E. S. Drower (E. J. Brill, Leiden, 1959).
DA	*Diwan Abatur*, trans. E. S. Drower, *Studi e Testi*, 151, 1950.
GR	*Ginza Rba*, trans. M. Lidzbarski (Göttingen, 1925). *GR*r (right side); *GR*l (left side).
H	*Clementine Homilies and Apostolic Constitution*, A–N Christian Library, vol. 17 (Clarke, Edinburgh, 1870).
J	M. Jastrow, *Dictionary of the Targumin, Talmud Babli, &c.* (Pardes, New York, 1950, 2 vols.).
JB	*Das Johannesbuch der Mandäer*, trans. M. Lidzbarski (Töpelmann, Giessen, 1915, 2 vols.).
JRAS	*Journal of the Royal Asiatic Society.*
MḏHZ	*Maṣbuta ḏ-Hibil-Ziwa*, trans. E. S. Drower, *Studi e Testi*, 176, 1953.
ML	*Mandäische Liturgien*, trans. M. Lidzbarski (Berlin, 1920).
MMII	E. S. Drower, *The Mandaeans of Iraq and Iran* (Clarendon Press, Oxford, 1937).
N	T. Nöldeke, *Mandäische Grammatik* (Halle, 1895).
OT	Old Testament.
ŠḏQ	*Šarḥ ḏ-Qabin ḏ-Šišlam-Rba*, trans. E. S. Drower, Biblica et Orientalia, no. 12 (Pontificio Istituto Biblico, Rome, 1950).
V	Vendidâd.
WW	E. S. Drower, *Water into Wine* (J. Murray, 1956).
ZDMG	*Zeitschriften der Deutschen Morgenländischen Gesellschaft.*

Note. The capital letter at the beginning of a word is a convention denoting a deity or god-like quality.

NOTE

THE Mandaic letter corresponding to the Hebrew ע and Arabic ع is transliterated by an inverted comma above the line, facing left. The first letter of the alphabet is transliterated by 'a'.

ACKNOWLEDGEMENTS

THE author would like to express gratitude to scholars who have helped her by various suggestions and corrections. Amongst these she names Professors H. Chadwick, E. R. Dodds, G. R. Driver, P. Kahle, A. Momigliano, and R. C. Zaehner. The list of helpers does not end there for it includes critical members of her own family, one or two friends, and the kind assistance of Mr. J. Thornton in procuring necessary books.

New evidence in Mandaean literature was, of course, the main reason for the helpful patience shown by those whom the author consulted whilst attempting to relate this hitherto unknown material to other gnostic literature, including the Khenoboskin *trouvaille*.

Finally, she would like to thank the staff of the Clarendon Press for their watchful care in shepherding the book through the press.

INTRODUCTION

BY the rivers of 'Iraq and especially in the alluvial land of Al-Khaur where the Tigris and Euphrates squander their waters in the marshes, meeting and mating at Qurnah before they flow into the Persian Gulf, and in the lowland of Persia along the Karun, which like its two sister rivers empties into the Gulf, there still dwells the remnant of a handsome people who call themselves *Mandaiia*, Mandaeans ('gnostics'), and speak a dialect of Aramaic. When the armies of Islam vanquished the Sassanids they were already there and in such numbers that the Qur'ān granted them protection as 'people of a book', calling them 'Ṣabaeans'. To that name they still cling, both in its literary form and as the vernacular *aṣ-Ṣubba*, for it ensures their existence as a tolerated community. The word (from ṢB', Syriac ܨܒܥ) means 'submergers' and refers to their baptism (*maṣbuta*) and frequent self-immersion. In the ninth book of his *Fihrist al-'ulūm*, Al-Nadīm, who wrote in the tenth century, calls them *al-Mughtasilah*, 'the self-ablutionists'.

I chose none of these names when writing of them in this book for, though this may appear paradoxical, those amongst the community who possess secret knowledge are called *Naṣuraiia*—Naṣoraeans (or, if the heavy 'ṣ' is written as 'z', Nazorenes). At the same time the ignorant or semi-ignorant laity are called 'Mandaeans', *Mandaiia*—'gnostics'. When a man becomes a priest he leaves 'Mandaeanism' and enters *tarmiduta*, 'priesthood'. Even then he has not attained to true enlightenment, for this, called 'Naṣirutha', is reserved for a very few. Those possessed of its secrets may call themselves Naṣoraeans, and 'Naṣoraean' today indicates not only one who observes strictly all rules of ritual purity, but one who understands the secret doctrine.

When the head priests of the community learned some years ago that two of their number had permitted certain scrolls to pass into my possession they showed resentment and anger. These scrolls, they said, contained 'secrets', knowledge imparted only to priests at ordination and never to laymen or to outsiders. Their attitude is understandable. When I was advanced enough in their language to read these documents, I found at intervals stern insistence on secrecy. Only 'one in a thousand and in two thousand two' would be found worthy of initiation into certain mysteries and any initiate who permitted them to become public was doomed to punishment in this world and the next.

The scrolls were of two kinds. In such manuscripts as 'A Thousand and Twelve Questions' (*Alf Trisar Šuialia*), the 'Diwan of Lofty Kingship' (*Diwan Malkuta 'laita*), the 'Great First World' and the 'Lesser First World' (*Alma Rišaia Rba* and *Alma Rišaia Zuṭa*), the teacher who hears and answers questions is an exalted spirit of light; these manuscripts are placed in the initiation hut when a novice is prepared for priesthood. The second type of 'secret' scroll, in which explanation of the mysteries is more or less incidental, is the *šarḥ*, a composition intended solely to instruct priests in the correct performance of ritual. The word means 'explanation, commentary'. Instruction usually takes the form of a description of a rite celebrated by spirits in the divine ether-world as a pattern for future priests in an as yet uncreated earthly world. The proper celebration of various types of baptism, *masiqta*, and Blessed Oblation are described in them. A third type of document provides scattered secret teaching, namely a codex containing the canonical prayers and canticles. As these codices are the personal property of priests and in constant use, it was many years before I could obtain a complete copy.

Only as manuscript after manuscript is studied does a picture gradually form of an ancient theosophy true to the type we call gnostic, which developed in the syncretistic centuries which preceded the fall of classical paganism. This theosophy was hybrid. It embraced the star-knowledge and wisdom of Babylon and Egypt, the dualism of Iranian sages and Plato, the high speculation of the Greeks, and the stern morality of Jewry and its book of books. Deeper roots may have reached yet farther east.

If one may venture into hypothesis, seedbeds in which Naṣirutha could well have germinated were the flourishing Jewish colonies in commercial towns in Parthia, Media, and Babylonia. These were, of course, in constant touch, not only with one another, but with Jerusalem. I suggest that such a sect may have spread into the Jordan valley, Galilee, and Judaea, where it would naturally have split into sub-sects, one of them possibly Christianity, which recognized in Jesus its crowned and anointed king—the Messiah. It is a striking fact that in all the Mandaean texts the word *mšiha* (Messiah, Christ) is only used with the qualification 'lying' or 'false' of Jesus, and this is the more surprising as every priest is a king (*malka*), crowned and anointed, as microcosm of the macrocosm Adam Kasia, the crowned and anointed Anthropos, Arch-priest, and creator of the cosmos made in his form. The word for the oil of unction is *miša* and the verbs for its application are RŠM and ADA. The implication is that the word *mšiha* (the anointed one) was so inextricably connected with the hated Jew and Christian that the root MŠH was banned from Naṣoraean use.

Having set foot on the slippery road of speculation, I assume that it might well follow that after the destruction of Jerusalem, when Jewish Christians for the most part settled in East Jordan, our Naṣoraeans, hating, and hated by, both Jew and Jewish-Christian, would naturally seek harbour in the friendlier atmosphere of Parthia and the Median hills—exactly as the *Haran Gawaita* relates, and, according to that manuscript ,a number of them migrated later under Parthian protection into Babylonia and Khuzistan. Did they find in the well-watered marsh districts there a baptizing gnostic sect like—or affiliated to—their own? It might explain much, but here I can only refer the reader to Chapter X of this book.

In the 'secret scrolls' Jesus and John are unmentioned. In the two codices accessible to the uninitiated (*GR* and Drašia-ḏ-

Yahia) the former is represented as a perverter of Naṣoraean teaching.

In contrast, when Jesus appears in the Coptic Christian gnostic manuscripts[1] he is used as a mouthpiece of *gnosis*. There is no attempt to represent him as an historical figure, although by use of his name the Coptic gnosis is given a Christian aspect. Dr. Gilles Quispel wrote recently:[2] 'Daß die Gnosis in Wesen und Ursprung *nicht* christlich ist wird immer klarer: ob sie aber vorchristlich ist, muß noch bewiesen werden.'

Naṣoraean scrolls of the first type mentioned on p. x exist in the libraries of head priests and are seldom copied, so that there is often a gap of several generations between one copy and the next.

To what date can they be ascribed? The genealogy of each composition is long: and in the colophons it is stated that such manuscripts when examined in the Moslem era were already ancient, fragmentary, and in places difficult to decipher. It is to be surmised that the arrival of proselytizing Islam into Mesopotamia and Persia startled Naṣoraeans and Mandaeans[3] in those countries out of sleepy complacency induced by the security they had enjoyed during the Seleucid, Parthian, and Sassanian epochs. Reformers, the liturgist Ramuia and his colleagues set about the task of collecting manuscripts, and, the colophons chronicle, travelled from place to place, from priest to priest, and from *bimanda* to *bimanda*[4] in search of them. The final result was a heterogeneous, but nevertheless canonical, literature. It should be remarked that the reformers showed little interest in setting theology to rights although the religion by the eighth and ninth

[1] e.g. in the Codex Askewianus and Codex Brucianus translated by Carl Schmidt, *Koptisch-Gnostische Schriften* (Leipzig, 1905), and in the *Evangelium Veritatis*, the first of the Khenoboskion papyri to be published. Judging by accounts given of the latter by M. Jean Doresse in *Livres secrets des gnostiques d'Égypte* (Plon, 1958), what I have said above would hold good for the remainder of these texts.

[2] *Gnosis als Weltreligion* (Origo Verlag, Zürich, 1951, p. 5).

[3] The two classes were at that time clearly defined as separate: the Naṣoraean belonged to the priestly clan and the Mandaean was a layman.

[4] *Bimanda* = *bit manda*, the name of the cult-hut or sanctuary of the Mandaeans.

centuries had become overgrown like a barnacled ship with a variety of contradictory tenets, additions, and legends. Reforming zeal was reserved for and concentrated upon the correct performance of ritual, the meticulous observance of ritual purity, and uniformity in the celebration of baptism and the sacraments. There followed an era of strict observance for priesthood and laity. Exact directions about the way in which the rites of the Naṣoraean church were to be performed were inserted in the canonical prayer book and a certain amount of literary activity ensued in the shape of *šarḥs* and such books as the *Haran Gawaita*, the *Diwan Abatur*, and other later compositions.

A considerable part of the surviving literature may be dated back to the earliest phases of Naṣoraeanism. Most scholars now accept Professor Säve-Söderbergh's discovery that the Coptic-Manichaean 'Psalms of Thomas' are adaptations, almost translations, of early Mandaic hymns,[1] not, as was hitherto supposed, vice versa. Al-Nadīm's story[2] that Fatik, Māni's father, belonged to the Mughtasilah sect is thereby strengthened, for there can be no doubt that this baptizing sect were Ṣābians, that is to say Mandaeans and Naṣoraeans.

Fresh presumptive evidence about the history of the sect came to light when I discovered and the Vatican Press published the *Haran Gawaita* just mentioned. It purported to be 'historical' and recounted in semi-legendary form how the Naṣoraeans fled from persecution in Jerusalem and sought refuge in the Median hills (*Ṭura ḏ-Madai*) and in *Haran Gawaita*, which I take to mean the city of Harran. Their persecutors were punished by the destruction of Jerusalem, which would place the flight before A.D. 70. In 'Haran' they found co-religionists and eventually migrated under a friendly Parthian king, Ardban (Artabanus), to Lower Mesopotamia where they established headquarters at a place called Ṭīb between Wāsiṭ and Khuzistan. Although this document cannot be accepted as a serious chron-

[1] Torgny Säve-Söderbergh, *Studies in the Coptic-Manichaean Psalm Book* (Uppsala, 1949), p. 128. The author suggests tentatively that the Mandaean hymns may be placed in the second century A.D. or earlier.

[2] In the *Fihrist-al-'Ulūm*, ed. G. Flügel (Leipzig, 1871–2, 2 vols.).

icle of events, it is of value as confirming oral tradition, for Mandaeans claim that they migrated into their present home from Harran and before that from Palestine. Most of the re-edited manuscripts were, according to the colophons, issued from Ṭīb.

Dr. Rudolf Macuch[1] points out that the sentence referring to Harran could be read 'in which there *are* Naṣoraeans', showing that, at the time at which the writer lived and wrote, Naṣoraeans, under that name, were still found in that city. Throughout the manuscript the word 'Naṣoraeans' is used, not 'Ṣābiya' (Ṣabians), and 'Mandaeans' are mentioned only once. The point raised here is discussed in the Appendix.

That Naṣoraeans were originally a Jewish group or partly Jewish group is suggested by their claim that John the Baptist was a member of their sect, and by the fact that the Jordan[2] is an essential and central feature of their tradition. Today the word *yardna* (jordan) is applied not only to running water used in baptism and immersion, but to any flowing stream; yet the conjunction of John the Baptist and the Jordan is significant. Epiphanius (*Adversus Haereses*, xxix: 6) says that there were 'Naṣoraeans' (*Νασαραῖοι*) amongst the Jews before the time of Christ.[3] The name could have been applied to any strictly law-observing Jewish sect, for the root נצר means 'to keep, observe, guard' and could have been used as a laudatory term for more than one group of Jewish dissidents, particularly if they had secret teachings.[4] Naṣoraeans of the Mandaean type 'keep and observe' ritual law with zealous fidelity and 'keep back'—even from their own laity—mysteries considered deep and easily misunderstood by the uninitiated.

Naṣoraean hatred for Jews must have originated at a period

[1] R. Macuch, 'Alter u. Heimat des Mandäismus nach neuerschlossenen Quellen', *Theologische Literaturzeitung* (June, 1957).

[2] The Jordan, in contrast to other rivers in Syria and Palestine, is never really cold, hence is peculiarly adapted for immersion at all times of the year.

[3] Lidzbarski (*ML*, p. xvii) makes short work of W. B. Smith's arguments in *Der vorchristliche Jesus* (Giessen, 1906) that Epiphanius was mistaken in this statement.

[4] Cf. Isaiah xlviii. 6 and lxv. 4, נְצֻרוֹת 'secret things' and נְצוּרִים 'secret places'.

at which Naṣoraeans were in close contact with orthodox Jewry and at a time when the orthodox Jews had some authority over them. All this points to the truth of the *Haran Gawaita* tradition. Heterodox Judaism in Galilee and Samaria appears to have taken shape in the form we now call gnostic, and it may well have existed some time before the Christian era. In the Schweich Lectures[1] given by Dr. Moses Gaster in 1923 on the Samaritans, the lecturer, speaking of settlements of Jews and Samaritans in the Diaspora, mentioned similarities which exist between Parseeism, Judaism, and Samaritanism, and pointed out the possibility that Mandaeism might also have sprouted in such seedbeds.

The figure of Pthahil and its connexion as demiurge with the Egyptian god Ptah (see p. 37, n. 2), the Mandaean tradition that they once had fellow religionists in Egypt,[2] and the apparently ancient belief transmitted by word of mouth that the dove slaughtered before the *masiqta* is called a *ba*[3] (unsatisfactory though these may be as evidence, for I can find little to justify them in the texts) must be considered contributory when assessing the possibility that Naṣirutha originated in semi-paganized Jewish circles.

In this book I have tried to view Naṣoraean gnosis as a whole, and have not concealed my belief that the secret teaching, based upon the Mystic Adam, goes back to the first or second centuries. Vitally significant aspects of that gnosis are evident in unpublished scrolls held as a closely-guarded heritage by the inner circle, the Naṣoraeans. These a layman, however pious, is not allowed to see or hear. They contain tenets imparted only to an initiated few; indeed, Naṣirutha could be called truly esoteric—a religion within a religion, a gnosis within a gnosis, and its heart is the interpretation which it attaches to sacramental acts.

[1] M. Gaster, *The Samaritans* (O.U.P. for the British Academy, 1925), p. 87.

[2] Until recently a *masiqta* was celebrated once a year for Egyptians drowned whilst chasing Moses and the Hebrews across the *yama ḏ-Suf*.

[3] The human-headed bird depicted in Egyptian tombs which represents the vital spirit, is called the *Ba*. See p. 8, n. 1.

To tabulate the principal features of the gnosis: Naṣirutha has preserved for us, as I shall try to convey in the following pages, a complete and coherent gnostic system. Its main features appear in various forms in other gnostic sects and they may be roughly summarized as these:

1. A supreme formless Entity, the expression of which in time and space is creation of spiritual, etheric, and material worlds and beings. Production of these is delegated by It to a creator or creators who originated in It. The cosmos is created by Archetypal Man, who produces it in similitude to his own shape.

2. Dualism: a cosmic Father and Mother, Light and Darkness, Right and Left, syzygy in cosmic and microcosmic form.

3. As a feature of this dualism, counter-types, a world of ideas.

4. The soul is portrayed as an exile, a captive; her home and origin being the supreme Entity to which she eventually returns.

5. Planets and stars influence fate and human beings, and are also places of detention after death.

6. A saviour spirit or saviour spirits which assist the soul on her journey through life and after it to 'worlds of light'.

7. A cult-language of symbol and metaphor. Ideas and qualities are personified.

8. 'Mysteries', i.e. sacraments to aid and purify the soul, to ensure her rebirth into a spiritual body, and her ascent from the world of matter. These are often adaptations of existing seasonal and traditional rites to which an esoteric interpretation is attached. In the case of the Naṣoraeans this interpretation is based on the Creation story (see 1 and 2), especially on the Divine Man, Adam, as crowned and anointed King-priest.

9. Great secrecy is enjoined upon initiates; full explanation of 1, 2, and 8 being reserved for those considered able to understand and preserve the gnosis.

Other features and developments occur in various syncretic and gnostic systems, but the above are, upon the whole, the distinguishing features of Naṣoraean gnosis, Naṣirutha.

I have not confined my quotations to the secret scrolls alone, for the *Ginza* (also called 'The Book of Adam', see 'Sources') and the liturgical prayers and canticles[1] are full of allusions to gnosis. One of the scrolls quoted,[2] a miscellany containing seven fragmentary books (at the time of writing it was still in page proof), will I feel certain be regarded as one of the most important Mandaean documents preserved for us in the priestly libraries. The style in which it and other manuscripts quoted are composed is obscure, perhaps intentionally so. The writers seem poor literary craftsmen: they dilate upon matters repellent to the Western mind, such as the organs and functions of the Body of the Secret Adam. To a Naṣoraean the human body is a replica of the glorious cosmic Body, the holiest of mysteries, and every organ in it, including those necessary to digestion, reproduction, and evacuation, has for him deep symbolical significance and is revered as an expression of the Divine chemistry of genesis, purification, and catharsis.

[1] *Mandäische Liturgien* (see 'Sources') contains about a third of the canonical book. A full and complete edition of the latter is now published under the title of *The Canonical Prayerbook of the Mandaeans* (E. J. Brill, Leiden).

[2] *Alf Trisar Šuialia* ('A Thousand and Twelve Questions'); see 'Sources'.

I

IN THE BEGINNING

> There was not the non-Existent nor the Existent then;
> There was not the air nor the heaven which was beyond.
> What did it contain? in whose protection?
> Was there Water, unfathomable, profound?
> *Rig-Veda*, x. 129 (Macdonell).

WHEN a playwright has his plot sketched out, his characters conceived, and his stage set— 'Let there be light!'—he takes his place, as it were, in the audience while those of whose existence he is the author work out the play before him. Often, indeed, his puppets develop in ways hardly intended, but the main plot is unaffected and the dramatist remains the supreme authority.

Such, on a cosmic scale, is the Naṣoraean concept of Existence emerging from non-Existence in the beginning. The Naṣoraean 'Author of Being', to use a Western phrase, is Existence *in excelsis*. It is absolutely without sex or human attribute and in speaking of It the pronoun 'They' is used, for *Hiia*, 'Life', is an abstract plural. Creation is delegated to emanations, and appeals are addressed to It by the two great creative forces which are the first manifestation of Itself, namely Mind—the instrument of evocation—and a personification of active Light, Ziwa or Yawar-Ziwa (Awaking, or Dazzling, Radiance). When Yawar is about to call into existence the 'ether-world' and spirits to inhabit it, he approaches the Author-Spectator as a suppliant, humbly: 'If it please You, Great Life; if it please You, Mighty Life!' seeking permission to begin his predestined task.

We find the ideas which Naṣoraean writers try to convey to us expressed in often contradictory terms. The picture changes, merges, melts before us as they envisage at an ever-fresh angle the *Parṣufa Rba*, the 'Great Immanence' or 'Great Countenance'—an epithet applied to the Great Life. Sometimes the

Cause seems to become the Causer or the Causer the Cause; the Thinker the Mind or the Mind the Thinker. The Great Life is described as *nukraiia*, literally 'alien', meaning 'remote, incomprehensible, ineffable'. The word used for 'Mind', *mana*,[1] is not in that sense Semitic but Iranian, suggesting that the word was first adopted under Iranian influence. A Naṣoraean hymn praises Yawar-Ziwa, the first Radiance which illumined the stage of existence, and the Mind which produced it:

I worship, praise and laud
The four hundred and forty-four names
Of Yawar-Ziwa son of 'Radiance-Appeared',[2]
King of 'uthras,[3] great Viceregent of shecinahs,[4]
Chief over mighty and celestial worlds
Of radiance, light and glory.
(He) who is within the Veil,
Within his own shecinah,
He, before whom no being existed.

Then I worship, laud and praise
The one great Name which is great,
The Name which is powerful.
Then I worship, laud and praise

[1] The word *mana* when meaning 'mind', 'thought', &c., is of non-Semitic derivation: the Aramaic *mana* is 'a garment', 'robe', 'vehicle', 'vessel', 'instrument'. There is often word-play on the two meanings, and this passed into other gnostic literature so that 'robe' or 'vessel' or 'vehicle' is used as a cryptogram for *mana* meaning 'mind' or 'soul'. For the Zend and Pehlevi meaning of *mana* see Nyberg, *Die Religionen des Alten Iran* (Mitteilungen der Vorderasiatisch-Ägyptischen Gesellschaft, Leipzig, 1938), p. 128. In general, *Mana* in a cosmic sense is equivalent to the Stoic, Valentinian, and Sethian *Νοῦς*, 'the emanation of the Forefather *προπάτωρ*'. Reitzenstein pointed out that the Valentinians translated the word *mana* as 'vessel' (its Aramaic meaning, possibly from a Mandaic source) when they made the dying soul exclaim: 'I am a precious vessel.' The double meaning, Aramaic and Iranian, appears to be used as a cryptogram in the gnostic 'Song of the Soul' (Acts of Thomas) when the Parthian prince meets his 'robe'. It is significant that Parthia is the home of the princely hero. Parthia is mentioned by Hippolytus and Irenaeus as the original centre of the Elkasaite heresy (see Chapter X).

[2] Nbaṭ-Ziwa, lit. 'Radiance burst forth'.

[3] An *'uthra* is an ethereal being, a spirit of light and life. 'Uthras were created when the ether-world came into being, see Chapter VII.

[4] A *škinta* (pl. *škinata*) is a 'dwelling', 'indwelling', 'shekinah', 'sanctuary'. The Mandaean cult-hut is called a *škinta* or *bimanda* (= *bit manda*).

That mystic First Mind [*Mana*]
The glory of Which was transmitted
Neither from the uttermost ends of the earth
Nor from gates within it.
For It is Mind, the Great, Mysterious, First,
The glory of which was communicated
By redoublings of radiance
And by intensification of light. (*CP* 374.)

The *Ginza* (*GR*r) describes creation as 'utterance', or 'a cry', 'a calling forth'. 'Through Thy Word' (*mimra*) says *GR*r 12, addressing the King of Light, 'everything came into being'. The first two pages of this book describe Supreme Life, the Great Life, in mainly negative terms. The 'great *Parṣufa*' has 'no associate to share Its Crown nor partner in Its rule'; It is 'light without darkness', 'the Life above the living', 'Glory above glories', 'Life without death', and so on. Such descriptions could be understood even by the uninitiated, but gnostic metaphor, the 'mystery idiom', appears from time to time in *GR*.

This is the Mystery and book of the Radiance which burneth in the *pihta*[1] which is effulgent in Its own radiance and great in Its light. (*GR*r 238.)

Pihta here does not mean as usual 'sacramental bread', but 'the opened', 'the revealed', used in the idiom of such mystery-hymns as 358–9 (*CP*) which begin, 'When He opened His Garment', referring to the first emanation and the act of creation; and in the word *lbuša*, 'garment', 'covering', 'cloak', we have a typical example of word-play on *mana* (see p. 2, n. 1), so that 'when He opened his *lbuša*' really means 'revealed His

[1] The roots PHT, PTH, and PTA mean 'to open', 'to break apart', and all are used sometimes to describe creative activity. PTA also means 'to originate'. Lidzbarski used the word *schuf* to translate *pta*. *Pihta* (lit. 'opened') is the ritual name of the loaf used at all sacred rites. It may mean 'something broken apart or into pieces' (see E. S. Drower, 'The Sacramental Bread (Pihtha) of the Mandæans', *ZDMG*, Bd. 105, Heft 1, 1955, p. 115, and cf. Aramaic פיתא). Bread is a symbol of life: the Arabic عيش 'life' also means 'bread' and 'wheat'.

Mind' or 'Thought'. In the first hymn the *mana* is mentioned directly afterwards:

For the First Mind (*mana*) began (*pta*) and dwelt therein.

Some words in the mystery-idiom are impossible to translate adequately, such as *tana* (Tanna?). Judging by the context in some passages it would seem to mean a matrix, a formative centre.[1] In the same hymn we hear of a *tanna* and it is mentioned in one of the baptismal hymns:

The Radiance glowed in great effulgence.
The *Tanna* dissolved and a *škinta* came into existence
And was established in the House of Life.

In *GR*r 238: 6 the *Tanna* is mentioned in a description of the creation of first things:

. . . and radiance issued from the *pihta*; light rested on the *pihta* and proceeded from it. It created an emanation for itself, the radiance and light which issued from itself. Radiance glowed, the light glowed; the *Tanna* heated, the *Tanna* dissolved.

The first prayer in the baptismal liturgy, the Book of Souls, begins thus:

In the name of the Life and in the name of Knowledge of Life and in the name of the Primal Being who was Eldest and preceded Water, Radiance, Light and Glory; the Being who cried with His voice and [*uttered*] Words. Vines grew and came into being and the First Life was established in its *škinta*. . . . The First Life is prior to the Second Life by six thousand myriad years, the second Life is prior to the Third Life by six thousand myriad years and the Third Life more ancient than any 'uthra [*spirit*] by six thousand myriad years. There is that which is infinite. At that time there was no solid earth and no inhabitant in the black waters. From them, from those black waters, Evil was formed and emerged.

Genesis i too includes 'waters' in the first act of creation. The Naṣoraean concept seems to be that the 'black waters' either existed already as a form of chaos, or accompanied the mani-

[1] It is sometimes personified.

festation of the Ineffable. Evil is depicted as the inevitable concomitant of matter: it appears as it were of itself as the result of the dualism which is the first expression of Unity in plurality. This inevitability appears again and again in the secret teaching:

For darkness and light are bound together: had there been no dark then light would not have come into being. (*ATŠ*, p. 134.)

The worlds of darkness and the worlds of light are Body [*'ṣṭuna*][1] and counterpart: they (complement) one another. Neither can remove from or approach the other, nor can either be separated from its partner. Moreover, each deriveth strength from the other. (ibid., p. 213.)

Other passages in the same scroll confirm the inevitability, the dependence of one upon the existence of the other:

O Vision of 'uthras, O Word from whose Mind all kings emanated! Behold! Light and Darkness are brothers; they proceeded from one Mystery and the Body [*'ṣṭuna*] retaineth both. And for each sign in the body [*pagra*][2] that pertaineth to Light there is a corresponding mark of Darkness. Were it not marked with the mark of Darkness it would not be established nor come forward for baptism and be signed with the Sign of Life. (ibid., p. 261).

Darkness and evil are almost synonymous, as in the Chinese YIN:

Reveal to me about Radiance [*ziwa*] and Light [*nhura*]; about Light and Darkness, Good and Evil, Life and Death, Truth and Error. (ibid., p. 211.)

[1] The word *'ṣṭun* or *'ṣṭuna* in Mandaic means (*a*) column, pillar, support, (*b*) trunk, body. It is used to designate the cosmic body of Adam Qadmaia, the Primal Adam, also called Adam Kasia, the mystic or secret Adam (see pp. 21 ff.). In the late Dr. Carl Schmidt's *Koptisch-Gnostische Schriften*, p. 335, a fragment from the Codex Brucianus (Unbekanntes altgnostisches Werk) in a passage which clearly refers to the Demiurge, the cosmic Adam, the 'second place' (τόπος) is allotted to the 'Demiurge, Father, Logos, Wellspring, Intelligence (Νοῦς) Eternal and Unending: this is the column (στῦλος) the Episkopos, the Father of all.' The passage reads like a translation from an Aramaic or Mandaic original and στῦλος (in spite of its original Sanskrit meaning) looks like a too literal translation of the West-Aramaic *'ṣṭun*. See p. 21, n. 1.

[2] The human body is usually called *'ṣṭun pagria* to distinguish it from Adam's 'Body'.

The answer is:

> Radiance [*ziwa*] is the Father and Light [*nhura*] the Mother; [*and of light and darkness*] . . . thou, Hibil-Ziwa art Light and Qin[1] is darkness. Between them I cast strife [yet] their voice is one, degrading or uplifting, urging to good or to evil. Good and Evil of which thou didst speak, I mingled together. They are living water and stagnant water, they are life and death, error and truth, wound and healing; they are Pthahil and Hibil-Ziwa, they are Spirit and Soul. (ibid., p. 211.)

The implication that *ziwa* (radiance is an approximate translation), the syzygy of *nhura*, is an active, creative male principle and light a receptive, passive (female) principle occurs more than once: in *ATŠ* Hibil-Ziwa says:

> Now as to these two mysteries of *ziwa* and *nhura*, know that they are the ancient Primal Father and Mother. Pure gold is the mystery [symbol] of the Father, its name is Radiance. Silver is the Mother's mystery [symbol] and its name is Light. The Crown is the Father's symbol and its name is Radiance: the myrtle-wreath the symbol of the Mother and its name is 'Let there be Light'. The 'owner of a crown' [*a priest*] is concerned with the mystery of the Father. A Mandaean [*i.e. layman*] and his wife are occupied with the mystery of the Mother.

The mutual interdependence and yet opposition in partnership is constantly expounded. The Teacher says (ibid., p. 145):

> Behold and learn that betwixt darkness and light there can be no union or pact: on the contrary, hatred, enmity and dissension, although We are aware of all that taketh place and seeketh to take place. For darkness is the adversary of light. They are Right and Left, they are *ruha* [vital spirit] and *nišimta* [soul]; moreover, they are called Adam and Eve.

Radiance, active light, was the first emanation. Its amplified name Yawar-Ziwa means 'dazzling' or 'awaking'[2] Light. The opening lines of a series of hymns (*CP* 358–69) are:

> When He opened His Garment and when Radiance was formed

[1] Qin; see p. 57, n. 1.

[2] For this form of the participle (in verbs the third radical of which is 'r' or 'l') see N, p. 230, par. 175, e.g. דאכאר.

or

When He opened the Garment of Life
And the radiance of the mighty Life appeared

continuing

To whom was Light given
And to whom was Enlightenment revealed?
Light was given to Yawar,
Light to Yawar was given.

and

Production was entrusted to Yawar,
To Yawar was [the task of] construction given.
He was created Chief of mighty ones:
He implanted reproductive power in his brethren.

Dualism is expressed in many ways and metaphors. The perpetual opposition and interdependence of two forces, like the negative and positive in electricity, combine to produce energy. Complementary pairs unite for the purpose: there are, in particular, the two who seem to symbolize the first 'sacred marriage' (and the pattern is repeated throughout the cosmos).

They are the *Aina usindirka*, the Wellspring and Date-palm. By modern Mandaeans the word *sindirka* is traditionally accepted as meaning both 'date-palm' (a male date-palm) and 'dates', and the *sindirka* which ritual texts order to be placed with other symbolic fruits on the altar table and eaten, to be crushed with grapes for the marriage drink, or pounded with sesame for the oil of unction at the *masiqta*, can be no other fruit.

Lidzbarski (*ML*, p. 28) translates the word as 'Palme' but says on p. xxi, 'Als Palme läßt sich סינדירכא nicht erklären', and after discussion of probabilities he concludes that the tree of Life may have been originally a juniper, and that the word *sindirka* must have come from the Persian for *sandarach* ('Im Persischen heißt سَنْدَرُوس und سَنْدَرَه das Harz des Wacholders'). The Mandaic word *sindarus* occurs often in ritual manuscripts (and in *GR*r 23); it is the perfumed resin used for incense, but transformation of *sindarus* into *sindirka* as meaning an edible fruit and a symbol of life seems dubious, especially as both words appear in close juxtaposition in descriptions of ritual.[1]

The choice of the date-palm as symbol of the Tree of Life and of male fecundity is justifiable on several counts. In Babylonia it served for a long time as a sacred emblem.[2] In Ephesus as symbol of fertility it figured in the temple of Artemis the many-breasted. The male date-palm with its fertilizing pollen, its upward-soaring shaft, naturally suggested a phallic symbol, and in the secret texts it is so explained in plain language. In the Middle East generally it was associated with nutrition and fertility. The ancient Egyptians knew it in this sense; for them it also symbolized the immortality of the soul and, like the part of the soul which was represented as a bird, it was called a *bai* or *ba*.[3] To add to the maze of trails—true or false[4]—in the courtyard of every Parsi fire-temple there must grow a date-palm and near it must be a well of flowing water, so that here we have in modern times wellspring and palm-tree side by side in a holy place. The well is a symbol of the Life from which all emanates and to which all must return (see *WW*, p. 221), and a strip of date-palm leaf is used by the Parsi *zoti* to bind the symbolic bundle of twigs which might be described, in the ancient Jewish phrase, as 'a bundle of life'. This parallel seems too close to be fortuitous. It suggests contact between people using such similes at one time or another and also syncretic ramifications far wider than hitherto assumed. Gnosis has been

[1] And the dove slaughtered as a symbol of the *ruha* before a *masiqta* is also called a *ba* by Mandaean priests. This name is traditional and part of the secret teaching, but confirmation in the texts is not forthcoming in any convincing form. A small fragment of the dove's flesh is placed on the *faṭira* which represents the departed spirit (*ruha*). The *sindirka* is mentioned with the *Mana* in the lead amulet strip in the British Museum: 'pronounce it in the strength of the *Mana* and *Sindirka*'. See *Ein mandäisches Amulett*, trs. by Mark Lidzbarski (Florilegium Melchior de Vogüé, Paris, 1909), pp. 364, line 177; 373, line 178.

[2] See Mrs. Van Buren, 'The Sacred Marriage', *Orientalia*, vol. 13, 1944, pp. 8–9.

[3] See p. xv, n. 3.

[4] See Prof. G. Widengren, *The King and the Tree of Life in Ancient Near Eastern Religion* (Uppsala, 1951), for Tree and Water of Life.

defined, by a disciple of Jung's school,[1] as 'mythische Projektion der Selbsterfahrung'. To some extent this is true: ideas are accepted only when they are in tune with inner convictions, but this does not rule out historicity or the development of ideas according to environment and contact.

Reference to the Wellspring and Date-palm is made in baptismal prayers. Whilst the candidate still stands in the water after his baptism, before he ascends the bank, the baptist lays his hand on the candidate's bowed head and pronounces the blessing known as 'the Names'. It begins:

The name of the Great Mystic First Wellspring be mentioned upon thee! The name of the Great First Palmtree (*sindirka*) be mentioned upon thee!

Throughout the canonical prayers this pair of creative and lifegiving powers are invoked in blessing. In *ATŠ* (p. 110) we have:

And the great and lofty One who is the Soul that sitteth in the celestial firmament spoke and said 'Praised be the First Great Radiance! I am Mara-ḏ-Rabutha, Father of 'uthras! Praised be the First Great Light, the Wellspring of Light, mother of the twenty-four letters of the alphabet, who is my Spouse. Praised be the Great First Wellspring and Date-palm, for the Date-palm is the Father and I, Mara-ḏ-Rabutha, was created by Him. Praised is the occult *tana*[2] which dwelleth within the great occult First Wellspring, for from that mystery of seed placed in the Jordan proceed all worlds and generations; fruit-trees, vines, trees, fish, winged birds, swarming creatures and sprouting growth. They drink thereof and are male and female: they become pregnant, increase and are multiplied. Praised be Šišlam-Rba[3] who sitteth on the bank of the Wellspring and Palmtree.'

... Then he said 'The Crown is composed of four mysteries, which are the Wellspring and Date-palm, Fecundation, Glory and Light.' (ibid., p. 117.)

And in the same book when the Great Mother had asked a question of the Father of 'uthras:

[1] Gilles Quispel, *Gnosis als Weltreligion*, p. 17. [2] See p. 4.

[3] The prototype of all priests (kings) and bridegrooms. See pp. 59 f.

Then the Father of 'uthras arose and hid himself in his Egg [House]. So the Great Mother arose; she went toward the Wellspring and Date-palm and hid herself. And she gazed and beheld the vines which stand beside the Wellspring, and fair was their fruit and their shade arching over the flowing stream. (ibid., p. 120.)

Then he taught about the Great Secret Wellspring, that She is the Womb, the Door of Mysteries through which kings have passed. Then he taught about the Great Primal Date-palm, that it is of Light and of the Body ['*ṣtuna*].[1] (ibid., p. 174.)

And in the description of the marriage of Šišlam to his heavenly bride 'zlat:

Then the Great First Father, the Pure Radiance, speaketh and saith to the guardian of *ginzia* [*mystic rites*], 'O great Guardian! Sublime and ineffable Vine! O good Vine! Turn thine eyes, view the Wellspring and Palmtree from whom Šišlam and 'zlat proceeded. Behold, these [two] have taken one another in marriage just as their Parents above did when their Father sought companionship and wished to create 'uthras.' (ibid., p. 267.)

Explanation of the cosmic pair is confined to the secret scrolls. The Diwan Malkuta 'laita explains bluntly that the Date-palm is a phallic symbol (see p. 8), and sexual metaphors and images employed by initiates are protected by special oaths of silence:

And be careful, be careful, three hundred and sixty times be careful, as I have warned you, in explanation of the Wellspring and Palmtree and [of] 'When I arose to My feet and when (as yet) I had created no Companion for Myself.' (Diwan Malkuta 'laita, lines 331 ff.)

Sex to the pious Mandaean is the holiest mystery of life and it is enjoined upon him to regard it as such and to pronounce the most sacred name, 'the great Life', before performing a sexual act. Continence is praised but celibacy is an unnatural and unholy state, condemned in the *GR*, especially in polemical passages referring to monasteries and convents.

[1] See p. 5, n. 1.

In the daily prayers, that pronounced at sunrise (*CP* 106) contains praise of the Divine and Cosmic Union:

> And praise great Yawar and 'zlat the Great,
> And praise Simat-Hiia [Treasure of Life] from Whom
> All worlds came into being.
> And praise the Wellspring and Datepalm
> From whom the Father of 'uthras came into being.

And in the important prayer known as the Šal Šulta (*CP* 171), the Divine Cosmic Marriage is typified in three allegorical pairs, Radiance and Light, Yawar-Ziwa and Simat-Hiia, and the Date-palm and Wellspring:

> Praised be the First great Radiance
> And praised the First great Light.
> Praised be the mystic Tanna
> Which dwelleth in the great mystic First Wellspring
> And the First Date-palm.
> Praised be the great 'zlat,
> Praised be the great Yawar who was formed
> From the loins of Radiance.
> Praised is Simat-Hiia, Mother of Kings,
> For from Her all worlds proceeded,
> Because She was appointed as the result
> Of secret mysteries.

II

THE FATHER AND MOTHER: THE ALPHABET

IN Naṣoraean cosmology the female principle of propagation, the Mother, is very like the Magian Spandarmat. As Professor Zaehner recently pointed out,[1] Spandarmat has a dual character:

They are aspects of one and the same principle, the eternal female, just as Ohrmazd and Ahriman are the two aspects of the eternal male.

Spandarmat is Mother Earth and she is also the 'Primal Whore'. The 'Mother' of Naṣoraean gnosticism is more than these, for in her highest aspect she is the divine Mother, complement of the Father. In her celestial character she has several aspects and several names: she is the 'Wellspring' (*Aina*), Mother of Life; she is Simat-Hiia, 'Treasure of Life', spouse of the great principle of divine enlightenment; she is 'zlat, archetype of pure Bride and she appears too as Naṣirutha, the true Naṣoraean faith. In the first and second aspects she is Mother of all spirits of life and light:

I am Mara-ḏ-Rabutha[2] [Lord of Greatness], Father of 'uthras; and the Wellspring is my Spouse. Praised is the great 'zlat for She is the wellspring of light: she is my Spouse, [mine], your Father, Mara-ḏ-Rabutha. . . . Praised be Treasure-of-Life, Mother of all worlds, She from whom the upper, middle and lower worlds emanated, for she is my Spouse, [*the spouse of*] Mara-ḏ-Rabutha, since her name is Naṣirutha. (*ATŠ*, p. 11.)

She is also the Earth-Mother, she is earthy and all that drags back to earth; she is *Ruha*[3] the personification of that part of

[1] R. C. Zaehner, *The Teachings of the Magi, a Compendium of Zoroastrian Beliefs* (Allen & Unwin, 1956), p. 69. 'Spandarmat is what Professor C. G. Jung and his school call the Great Mother.'

[2] This also means the 'Lord of Teaching', which is one of the names given to Adam Kasia in his character of archetype of priest-initiator.

[3] *Ruha*, see p. 47.

human character which loves frivolity, dancing, sons, and the lusts of the flesh. When a man becomes a priest he must divest himself of the Mother and 'put on the Father', in other words, must put off that which is earthly and identify himself with that which is spiritual. In one aspect she resembles the Indian Kali: she produces and nourishes her children but she also devours them:

Behold, everything is founded in the Earth and issueth from her and is kept in her and there is nought which leaveth her save soul and spirit which the Jordan bringeth out from her and delivereth them from her snares and bonds. For Earth is Ruha who holdeth and entangleth all mysteries and any being who doth not seek to depart from her.

Behold this fair body that was nurtured by her! [*At death*] she encloseth it and consumeth it and maketh it as if it had never existed. And all the kindly mysteries which she produces and tends as [*one tends*] a lamp with oil, eventually she turns on them and devours them with teeth of wrath. This is the Earth of the Parents. She raised up physical life and she is the Great Mother from Whom all swarming creatures, burgeonings and increase proceeded and by Whom they are maintained. (*ATŠ*, pp. 238–9).

The Mother is 'the Left', the Father 'the Right': the Mother, Earth, the Father, Sky; the Mother, Matter; the Father, Non-matter; the Mother, *ruha* (vital spirit), and the Father, *nišimta* (soul). Their union is necessary for creation, it is necessary for life here and for life hereafter:

For the Drop [*Niṭufta*][1] of the Father and the [*Womb of the*] Mother are ranged with spirit and soul in the body. For the Drop combineth two mysteries and they are the mystery of the Father and of the Mother [*as was*] explained concerning them. Further, two mysteries, spirit and soul, came into being, were formed, and were called 'the four mysteries'. So Drop and Drop grasped one another's mysteries and solidification took place in the Womb.

And no body [*'ṣṭuna*] can exist that is not born [*conceived*] by two mysteries and built up of four mysteries. And when the four have

[1] *Niṭufta*, lit. 'drop', a personified drop of 'water of life', the semen or seed of the Father.

given it shape, seven arise and subdivide into nine and then twelve shine forth in it.[1] And [in] sixty days sixty seals are set on it. Thirty days set on it the seal of the Father and thirty nights set the seal of the Mother on it until it is given over to one of them.

If the Father signeth it in the Jordan it becomes the Father's: if the Mother signeth it in fire, it becomes the Mother's. It will belong to the one of the twain who signed it and there will be no hatred, rancour or dissension between them on account of what they said and did.

Covenant and boundary were made so that neither should be antagonistic to the other. So it is like a house, for building which design was employed. 'House' is its name, for everything proceeded from it and was formed in it.

Thus the whole earth is a house: it is a great house in which mysteries are kept and selected by test. It is an Egg of Life [House of Life] for the Great Father. (ibid., pp. 182–3.)

The primal union of the cosmic pair took place at the Beginning:

And He took a Spouse for Himself and created plants[2] and created worlds. (ibid., p. 118.)

There are those who delight in the Father and those who delight in the Mother. Those dedicated to the Father belong to the portion of the Right and those dedicated to the Mother to the portion of the Left. They are two *malkia* [lit. 'kings', ruling powers]: the one was begotten by the *Parṣufa* [*but*] fell downward and the other begotten by the lower and rose upwards. (ibid., p. 201.)

The Father is sometimes equated with Ayar (Ether), or with epithets, Ayar-Rba (Great-Ether) and Ayar-Ziwa (Ether-Radiance). Ayar (Ether) is the first attentuated pure element in which spirits exist, move, and have their being. It is the rarest of all elements: the 'most thin air' of the Essenes.[3] It interpene-

[1] This passage recalls one in the Jewish *Sefer Yeṣirah* describing creation: 'one over three, three over seven, seven over twelve and all of them attached (*aduqin*) to one another'.

[2] 'Plants' are symbolically 'plantings of life', life transferred from one place to another: hence children, pupils, and so on.

[3] Josephus, *Wars of the Jews*, bk. II, viii. 11 (Whiston, Edinburgh, n.d.). 'For their doctrine is this: "that bodies are corruptible and that the matter of which they are made is not permanent: but that souls are immortal and

trates the grosser air round the earth and purifies it. It is related to the Vayu of the Zoroastrians and *Rig-Veda*. It was the all but first, or at any rate a very early emanation. In *CP*, Prayer 233, Yawar-Ziwa,[1] who in the poem is called 'the proven, pure One', reports its creation which was necessary before the creation of the 'uthras[2] who would inhabit the 'ether-world':

> In it Radiance [*ziwa*] will form itself
> And sublime Light [*nhura*] be set up therein.
> In it there will be 'uthras[2]
> And Rays-of-Light will be established therein
> Appearances that shine with lovely radiance.

In the ritual manuscripts describing the celebration of heavenly mysteries, Ayar (or Ayar-Ziwa or Ayar-Rba) is given the role of chief celebrant, corresponding to that of a *ganzibra*[3] or head priest on earth. Ayar is the personification of a divine and absolutely pure atmosphere, the very essence of Life drawn into the light-body by something akin to breathing. The soul brings it with her into the world. We hear also of *ayar baraia*, 'the outer ether', and *ayar gawaia*, 'the inner ether', the latter probably meaning the breath or pure air of Life within the soul.

> We send them [*i.e. human beings*] pure ether that will build up their fabric and sweeten their stink. [*But*] they are ungrateful to the Life and complain that it is [*too*] cold and strong. And We send them living waters, bright and invigorating, that they may live and be raised up by them. [*But*] they go not down into them [*in baptism*], nor do they receive the Pure Sign. (*ARR*, lines 221 f.)

In *ATŠ*, p. 173, we find:

> The outer Ether is held above the skies and exists below the earth. Corporate creatures and trees [*it hath none*] and fish do not move

continue for ever; and that they come out of the most subtile air and are united to their bodies as in prisons . . . but that when they are set free, they then, as released from a long bondage, rejoice and mount upward."' Αἰθήρ is said by Epiphanius (*Haer.* xix. 1 and xix. 6) to be one of the seven witnesses necessary for an Elkasaite oath, see A. J. H. W. Brandt, *Elchasai: ein Religionsstifter u. sein Werk* (Hinrichs'sche Buchhandlung, Leipzig, 1912), pp. 15–16.

[1] The name of the first cosmic light, see p. 2.

[2] Spirits of life and light who inhabit the world of ideal counterparts.

[3] See *MMII*, p. 169.

about in ether-water: they can neither subsist nor travel therein because it is the sublime ether-atmosphere in which kings hold council. And they hold to it because they call it *qina* ['*nest*', '*home*'], since the mysteries are nurtured therein.

The personified Ether is self-emanated, a *malka ḏ-mn nafšh̲ praš*. He is also a teacher: in the *ARR* he not only acts as chief celebrant in celestial rites but explains their purpose and secret meaning. The soul for whom these 'pattern rites' are performed is that of Adam-Shaq-Ziwa, i.e. Adam Qadmaia, the Primal Adam who is the archetype of the yet unborn humanity. A passage illustrating this is quoted in a later chapter. In the Diwan Malkuta 'laita (lines 165–76), in a passage describing the 'pattern' initiation of a priest, candidates for the crown of priesthood are questioned by the examining board of spirit-priests:

> 'Tell us about the mystery of the *ruha* [spirit] and the mystery of the *nišimta* [soul]. Tell us who is thy Father and who thy Mother!' And they [*the novices*] reply 'My Father, our Father, is Ether and our Mother is the Jordan.'[1]

When (see *CP*. Hymn 239) Yawar-Ziwa with a mandate from the Great Life had called into being the 'ether-world', the other sacred element was still uncreated. 'In the Ether there is no water: how can the 'uthras thrive?' he asks. The 'Great Predestinate' then created the heavenly Jordan or, rather, Jordans of water of Life, for baptism was celebrated in the world of perfection.

> They created a store of living waters [*water of Life*]
> They let it flow down to the ether.
> They sent it down, caused it to flow down
> To the ether, to the dwelling of 'uthras.
> All of them savoured it and it was fragrant:
> All 'uthras savour it and it pleaseth.
> The 'uthras all drank and throve.
> They drank and rejoiced thereat
> And into their hearts Naṣirutha was poured. (*CP* 239.)

[1] The '*Aina* (Wellspring) in her celestial aspect becomes the Jordan.

We will now turn to the alphabet.

The Jewish *Sefer Yeṣirah* purports to be a Book of Creation. Professor Scholem[1] thinks it may have been composed between the third and sixth centuries. He writes:

... the elements of the world ... are sought in the ten elementary and primordial numbers—Sefiroth, as the book calls them—and the 22 letters of the Hebrew alphabet. These together represent the mysterious forces whose convergence has produced the various combinations observable throughout the whole of creation; they are the 'thirty-two secret paths of wisdom' through which God has created all that exists.

Such a concept appears repeatedly in the secret Mandaean texts when they describe the process of forming the universe into anthropomorphic shape. It is the kind of allegory which would appeal to priestly scribes and rabbis and its origin may be sought in schools of thought influenced by Pythagoras. In all gnostic writings the 'Word' (*logos*) is full of creative power, for the act of pronunciation was the act of creation. The Word 'existed with God' says St. John the Evangelist, and 'was God'. In Mandaic it is the *mimra* or *malalta*, the spoken Word. As 'Mahzian-the-Word' it is sometimes personified as a messenger who brings divine decisions to the 'uthras.

To pronounce or write a name in magic is to summon its owner. The Idea is the first stage of conception: speaking aloud (i.e. the 'word') is the next, and it gives the idea shape and existence. The written word, therefore, has magical, mystical, and holy power and the belief that it has reflects the awe in which the unlettered hold the lettered. And each letter in a word has, in itself, dynamic virtue, both numerical and magical.[2] This may account for the presence in some gnostic writings of seemingly nonsensical names. Mandaeans wear letters as charms and I was told that some of them place the alphabet under their pillows at night as a protection against evil. Most Mandaean

[1] G. Scholem, *Major Trends in Jewish Mysticism* (Thames & Hudson, 1955), p. 76.

[2] Alphabet magic and the magic of secret names is Oriental rather than Greek in origin. See B. L. van der Waerden, 'Das Große Jahr und die ewige Wiederkehr', *Hermes*, lxxx (1952), 129 ff., and 'Das Große Jahr des Orpheus', ibid., lxxxi (1953), 481 ff., who quotes the Greek and Oriental sources.

talismans begin with a list of the twenty-two, or as they would say twenty-*four*, letters of the alphabet, for to bring the number to the solar 24, the first letter is repeated at the end and the particle '*d*' inserted. The Aleph is represented by a circle, symbol of perfection, or of Life unending, and of the sun-disk as light on earth. With this symbol of divine perfection (the 'Alpha and Omega') the alphabet begins and ends, so that in itself the alphabet symbolizes the return of all things to their Source.

Hence, when creation is described in the secret books, the symbolism of the alphabet is utilized, and no doubt the mystics who teased hidden allusions out of such passages spent many an hour in meditation and in discussion about them.

In a hymn in *ATŠ* (which seems to be a variation of the Šal Šulta, see p. 11), the alphabet is included in a paean about creation.

And the great and Lofty One[1] who is the Soul who sitteth in the celestial firmament spoke and said 'Praised be the Great Radiance! I am Mara-ḏ-Rabutha, Father of 'uthras. Praised be the great First Light, the Wellspring of Light, *mother of the twenty-four letters of the alphabet*, who is my Spouse. Praised be the great first Wellspring and Date-palm, for the Date-palm is the Father and I, Mara-ḏ-Rabutha, was created by Him. Praised is the occult Tanna which dwelleth within the great occult First Wellspring. For from that mystery of Seed placed within the Jordan proceed all worlds and generations—the fruit-trees, vines, trees, fish, winged birds, swarming creatures and sprouting growth. They drink thereof and are male and female: they become pregnant, increase and are multiplied. Praised be Šišlam-Rba[2] who sitteth on the bank of the Wellspring and Palmtree.' . . . (*ATŠ*, pp. 110–11.)

In a description of the first assumption of the crown of priesthood in the ether-world, Adam-Kasia—as Mara-ḏ-Rabutha—had none to initiate him or teach him, since He Himself is Initiator and Teacher.

So when He, the Father of 'uthras, formed Himself and was manifest, He came into being and went down; He sent (?) and rested

[1] The secret teaching explains this as Adam Kasia. [2] See pp. 59 f.

upon the well Šarat,[1] Hag and Mag[2] is its name, Zahriel[3] is its name, Bihram[4] is its name. And within it dwell the three hundred and sixty thousand mysteries from which She, the Wellspring, emanated.

And He enunciated the alphabet [ABGD] and put His proficiency to test therein: he studied and plumbed its height and its depth. And He recited the Book of Souls and all books.[5]

Another mystical and obscure passage in the same book represents the letters of the alphabet[6] as instrumental in forming Primal Man (Adam Kasia), the cosmos in the shape of physical Man.

And so, when they beheld the mysteries of their Nest [*i.e. home, origin*], they understood and each of them individually took itself in hand until they were in order and knew whither they were tending. And the mysteries of the Right governed themselves and knew that the mysteries of the Left had expressed themselves.[7] And so, as they perceived, at this point there was division.

The 'L' came into being—and up to the 'La' they were twelve. And from the halfway 'La' unto the end of the living [*mysteries?*] it was [*also*] twelve because they divided that Well in which there are four corners. Thus its counterpart which pertaineth to it, which is named 'L', is seen to be the middle half of the alphabet.

When they were 'H' the mysteries expressed themselves defectively but encouraged themselves saying, 'If we separate ourselves and place ourselves at a distance one from the other the building will not hold together. [But] if we approach one another and merge together we shall construct the building soundly and will set it out in orderly fashion. We shall eat of His bounty. And when each of us is set in order in the building He will assume the principal part. If we do not join with one another the Right will be useless, the Left ruined and the mouth (opening) of every one of the mysteries will be spoilt.'

[1] Lit. 'it ran over, swelled, rose (overflowed)'. שָׁאַר.

[2] The name of a pair of rulers in the underworld: the reference, I suppose, is to the visit of Hibil-Ziwa to that world in search of the *gimra*, see pp. 57 f.

[3] See p. 58.

[4] See p. 65.

[5] Candidates for priesthood are examined by a board of priests before they receive the 'crown' and must be able to recite the Book of Souls (baptism liturgy) by heart, and to read or recite from other holy books.

[6] This passage should be compared with the Marcosian theory of letters as quoted by Hippolytus, *Refutation of all Heresies*, bk. vi, trans. by J. H. Macmahon, A-N Christian Library (Clarke, Edinburgh, 1868, 2 vols.), vol. i, p. 261.

[7] Or 'had separated themselves'.

When they had thus regarded themselves, they took hold of one another's hands at those corners and set their course towards Him. And He turned about in His kingliness and caused them to approach Himself, gave His testimony and set them to work on the House. (*ATŠ*, pp. 181 f.)

The obscurity of this and similar passages makes difficult the task of the translator who is anxious to avoid distortion through paraphrase. (In comparison to the Jewish *Sefer Yeṣirah* it is crystal-clear!) An equally dark passage occurs in another fragment in the same collection: this concerns the mystic marriage of Šišlam-Rba to the great 'zlat:

This is the Wellspring from which Naṣirutha[1] emanated and was distributed amongst the *škinata.*[2] She convinced 'uthras and drew kings [*priests*] to Naṣirutha in their minds. And 'uthras and kings say to the Great First Father, the Hidden Radiance, 'We entreat Thee to explain to us this Well of the ABGD[3] from which all animals, cattle, fish, winged fowls; all burgeoning plants, flowing streams [*yardnia*] and rays of light burst into life. And Ether spoke in the ABGD but did not come forth from the ABGD. What is its depth? what is its height? How great is its extent and how many were the upsurgings which sprang forth from it? For there is not one of the kings who knoweth about it—[*yet*] any king who doth not testify about it [*according to*] Naṣirutha will not be established with kings in the Light.

'O Father, Hidden Radiance, Light that is mightier than the worlds! Teach us so that our understanding may make it clear to us and our hearts be doubly reassured. Therefore teach us about propagation and increase, about the first great [*Act of*] Reproduction by which propagation is propagated.'

[1] The secret teaching of Naṣoraeans.

[2] *Škinta*, see p. 2, n. 4.

[3] Every letter of the alphabet is a 'crown': 'And he said "The 24 letters of the ABGD are twenty-four crowns worn by 24 kings who were formed of light"': Diwan Malkuta 'laita, line 621.

III

ADAM KASIA, THE SECRET OR HIDDEN ADAM

The first man (Adam) became a living soul. (Gen. ii. 7.)
The first man, Adam, became a living soul: the last Adam was made a quickening spirit. (1 Cor. xv. 45.)

ON pp. 5 and 10 there are references to the *'ṣṭuna*. The word *'ṣṭun* or *'ṣṭuna* in Mandaic (ܐܣܛܘܢܐ Syriac) means 'the trunk' (of a human body), or 'a column, support'. When used of a cosmic being the word means the former, not the latter.[1]

The Body (and for the sake of clarity I will give it a capital 'B' to distinguish it from 'body' which in Mandaic is usually *pagra* or *'ṣṭun pagria*) is that of Adam Qadmaia,[2] the 'First

[1] See p. 4, n. 1. In the *Fihrist* (see Flügel's edition) the Manichaean 'column of Glory' is rendered عمود السبح. It is quoted by Prof. Widengren as such in *The Great Vohu Manah* (Uppsala, 1945), and by Dr. Mary Boyce in *The Manichaean Hymn-Cycles in Parthian* (Oxford Univ. Press, 1954), p. 20. By it, souls ascended to the world of light (as in the Mandaean *masiqta*). Widengren points out (op. cit., p. 14) that this 'column' is always associated with the 'Perfect Man' (i.e. the First Adam). Dr. Boyce writes to me that ''*ṣṭun* is an Indo-Iranian word: Sanskrit *sthuṇa*, Avestan *stūna*, Manichaean Middle Persian *istun* and Persian *setūn*. The Syriac is *'sṭwn'* (all of which undoubtedly mean 'pillar, column'). In the case of Adam, whose body stands erect, the *'ṣṭun* (as in other Mandaic texts) has the meaning of 'body', i.e. without the head and limbs, body in a literal sense of trunk. In Manichaeanism the Milky Way was called the 'Pillar' of Glory (Parthian *b'm 'stwn*), a conception which could well have been derived from the Light-Body of the cosmic Adam. According to Dr. Boyce 'the Last Man''s body was composed of the last particles of light to be saved from earth at the end of the world. The Manichaean doctrine is evidently a development of the Naṣoraean concept of the cosmic Man.

[2] 'According to the Jewish mystics God first created the Heavenly Man, the Archetype, who filled the universe and served as the pattern on which it was made' (H. Schonfield, ed., *The Authentic New Testament* (Dobson, 1956), p. 309, n. 59.) He is the Adam Kadmon of Lurianic Kabbalism: 'Adam Kadmon is nothing but a first configuration of the divine light which flows from the essence of *En-Sof* into the primeval space' (G. Scholem, *Major Trends in Jewish Mysticism*, p. 265). A useful study of the *Urmensch* is Kurt Rudolph's 'Ein Grundtyp gnostischer Urmensch-Adam-Spekulation', *Zeitschrift für Religions- u. Geistesgeschichte*, ix. Jahrgang, 1957, p. 1.

Adam', Adam Kasia, the Mystic or Secret Adam who preceded the human Adam called *Adam pagria* (physical man) by many myriads of years, for the macrocosm preceded the microcosm and the Idea of the cosmos was formed in human shape, so that through the creation of the one the creation of the other ensued. In like manner, according to the secret doctrine, as we shall see in a later chapter, it is through and because of Adam Kasia that a disembodied soul obtains its spiritual body. The detailed description of the construction of Adam Kasia's Body is understood when the ritual manuscripts are read, for every act in the *masiqta* is represented as part of the process by which the new and spiritual body is built up for the departed soul from plasma to perfection within the cosmic Womb.

As Primordial Man he is a gnostic figure rather than a purely Jewish or Iranian concept.[1] Explanations about Adam and his (the cosmic) Body are secret:

> For this mystery, this explanation, is a Voice which explaineth voices, a Word which interpreteth all words: it is [like] a good man who teacheth and addresseth each individually. It is the cry that was called at dawn and the last cry uttered at night. For with it emerged perception: it made a pronouncement which confounded all other pronouncements. And it progressed and ascended to its rightful place. (*ATŠ*, p. 168.)

Because Adam is the All, and comprises in himself every spiritual manifestation of the Great Life as well as the universe,

[1] As Primordial Man the Naṣoraean Adam has much in common with the Zurvanic 'Endless Form' which contained both the ideal and the material creation. See R. C. Zaehner, *Zurvan* (Clarendon Press, Oxford, 1955), p. 127. The Greater Bundahišn, quoted on p. 318 of the same book, describes the gradual building up of the cosmic being in terms which are remarkably close to those used in the Naṣoraean secret scrolls of the development of the embryonic Adam in the womb of the cosmic Mother. If the cosmos was built in the form of Primordial Man, the converse follows: man, the microcosm, is built up in form of the cosmos. This belief was Hermetic also. 'Hermès se représente l'homme comme un microcosme, tout ce que contient le macrocosme l'homme le contenant aussi. . . . Le macrocosme a des fleuves, des sources, des mers: l'homme a les entrailles', &c. (A. J. Festugière, O.P., *La Révélation d'Hermès Trismégiste* (l'Hermétisme et l'astrologie), Paris, 1950, p. 127.)

the mystic who tries to convey this multiple personality often becomes confused in his attempted explanation.[1]

Then he taught about Adam, whom all the worlds call Adam and in all the books they call him Adam, Adam is his name. Then he said 'I am the Adam of the mighty Life. I am Adam [*son*] of the Mighty Life for I shine in praise of my Father. Know that when Adam was united with Hawa [Eve], Adam was the Soul and Eve Body, and she is the Earth and Adam the Sky. Behold, a name was assigned to them when they inaugurated the mysteries of kings and put on the Body and bore children and propagated generations.' (ibid., p. 173.)

The physical man, *Adam pagria*, came into being through the union of the cosmic pair.

When they beheld children by divining [*or testing*] mysteries, Adam and Šitil [Seth] came into being, and yonder they called Seth 'the mysteries of the soul' and they called Adam 'the body', because in that Place Adam was the blood and Seth was the soul. And in another sense, Adam was darkness of the eyes and Seth was vision, and Adam was Earth whilst in all the mysteries Seth is the Jordan, for all of them are connected with the Jordan. (ibid., p. 173.)

The first creative impulse, when the Great Life became active and Non-Existence became Existence,[2] assumed an anthropomorphic shape. The explanation of this is given by Naṣirutha in theological rather than metaphysical language.

In the name of the great powerful *Mana* [Mind]
Who thought and evoked companionship for Itself
And said 'There shall be companionship for Me.' (*CP* 375.)

The *ARR* (line 24, rt. side) relates in haggadic form the calling forth of the First Adam from the Wellspring—the Womb of Creation. The task is deputed to the cosmic Light, Yawar-Ziwa, who speaks first of his own emergence from the two great generative forces, the Male and Female:

[1] G. Quispel has exactly expressed the Naṣoraean concept of Adam in *The Jung Codex and its Significance* (Mowbrays, London, 1955), p. 77: 'That Adam is the All is clear from a passage in *Yalkuth Shimoni* on *Genesis*, para. 34: "He cast a soul into him and set him up comprising in him the universe."'

[2] 'Nothing was when He (or It) was not and nothing would be were He not to be' (*GR*r 5).

Then was I formed from the Wellspring and Palmtree [Date-palm], I, the King who is All-Light. And a thousand thousand years, years countless and endless, passed until I planned to create offspring [lit. 'plants']. Then spake the Father saying to me, 'O lofty King, O Tree in whose shade they will sit! Arise, call forth sons who will be called "kings".'[1] . . .

The creation of Adam is related in the third person, and it begins, like all divine acts, with immersion (i.e. baptism?) and prayer. As *kušṭa*[2] is in the Naṣoraean church a rite which must precede and conclude every sacramental rite, personified Ether is called upon to be present for the ritual handclasp symbolical of truth and good faith.

And he [Inner-Ether] stretched forth his hand and placed it in the hand of the King-who-is-all-Light and said to him '[Let] Truth strengthen and stablish thee' [*Kušṭa asiak uqaimak*]. And he said to him 'Seek and find, speak and be heard! The 'uthras whom thou hast worshipped shall be to thee helper, support and saviour in the Great Place of Light and Everlasting Abode.'[3]

Then the mouths of sixty wellsprings were opened and with one voice they began to bless and make obeisance to him. And they hymned him and cried to him

'In the name of the Life!
On the day that He was revealed:
On the day that Truth [*kušṭa*] was defined
Light was enhanced by the Jordan,
Light shone forth and was mighty.
It was imparted to kings
And kings were instructed in the Sign[4]
And were fortified and waxed exceeding great.'

Creation of the First Adam follows:

[1] By 'kings' priests are always meant, or 'uthras who prefigure the priesthood.

[2] *Kušṭa* ('truth, troth, pact, sincerity'). The act of exchanging the ritual handclasp is symbolical of good faith and of covenant.

[3] A quotation from the baptism liturgy. The baptizer grasps the hand of the person whom he baptized. The initiation formula ('Seek and find', &c.), is said on various occasions, e.g. initiation into priesthood. The ritual handclasp is part of the sacrament for the dying ('the Letter').

[4] 'The Sign' is baptism.

Then He stood at the brink of the Wellspring and Date-palm and gazed into the Wellspring and beheld therein that which is wondrous. Then the Seed formed within the Wellspring and [=*for*] He had planned to create Adam His eldest Son, whom the worlds worship and from whom a host [*of beings*] multiplied and came into existence for Him.

And He then rose to His feet and said 'In the name of the Great Life answer me and uplift me, [O] Great One, Son of the Mighty [Life]. Uplift me!' And He [*the Mana* ?] replied, 'O, My good Offshoot, what seekest thou?' And He said to Him 'I seek to create sons'. [Thus] then was Seed cast and fell into that Wellspring which is called the Womb. There it remained for three hundred and sixty days until everything had become strong.

Then there was sent to it the lofty force which is named pure ether [*Ayar-dakia*]—it hath three hundred and sixty names, three hundred and sixty wings and three hundred and sixty aspects [*parṣufia*]. (ARR, lines 67 ff.)

When he emerges from the Well of Creation Adam Qadmaia is taught his greatness and his smallness, for he is both macrocosm and microcosm:

And he [Adam] ascended the bank of the Wellspring and his glory burst forth over all worlds. Then he arose and sat by a well of vain imaginings and said 'I am a king without a peer! I am lord of the whole world!'[1]

He travelled on into all the world until he came and rested on a mountain, then he gazed about and perceived a stream coming from beneath the mountain. Then he prostrated himself, cast himself down on his face and said 'Is there a loftier and mightier than I? This is a Stream of living waters, white waters which come from worlds without limit or count!' Then his mind became disquieted. He pondered and said 'I said that there was no king greater than I, [but] now I know that there exists That which is greater than myself. I pray that I may see Him and take Him for my Companion.'

[1] Irenaeus, *Against Heresies.* bk. i, xxx, trans. by A. Roberts and W. H. Rambaut, A-N Christian Library (Clarke, Edinburgh, 1868, 2 vols.), vol. i, p. 106, on the Ophites: 'Yaldabaoth, becoming uplifted in spirit, boasted himself over all things that were below him and exclaimed "I am Father and God, and above me there is no-one".' Valentinus makes his Demiurge utter a similar cry. Vaunts recalling Isa. xlv. 5–6 and xlvi. 9 occur no less than five times in the Coptic Khenoboskion papyri: they are uttered by a demiurge or other created cosmic being (pp. 172, 182, 184, and 222 of Professor Doresse's summarized version of these manuscripts).

Then a Voice came from above at which he fell upon his face and was powerless to rise and [stayed] fallen on his face until Ayar-Dakia [Pure-Ether] came—and in his right hand he was carrying a Letter.[1]

Then he [Adam] took the Letter into his right hand, smelt at it, sneezed,[2] prayed and praised the King Who is all Light and said 'I beseech Thee for lofty strength like Thine own.'

Then a Voice came to him from above and it sent Mahzian-the-Word. In his hand he was carrying a Letter. And he came towards him and gave the Letter into his [Adam's] right hand and he [Adam] kissed it three hundred and sixty times, then opened it, but understood not what was in it. He rejoiced in his mind and prostrated himself before Mahzian-the-Word and thereafter arose and understood the ABG and comprehended all Naṣirutha little by little.

This allegory shows Primal Man, His pride in Himself shorn away by the sight of Water of Life, learning from Mahzian-the-Word (here this might foreshadow written revelation) the rites which in the future physical World, He, and human celebrants in future ages mirroring himself, must perform.

The First Adam is a vast shape[3] embracing all that is to exist in the future cosmos. As the First Priest he is identified in one fragment of the *ATŠ* with Mara-ḏ-Rabutha, and he sets on himself the crown of priesthood, which is the crown of intermediation between the worlds of light and those of matter, himself. The ecclesiastical test for literacy and knowledge of the holy books is pre-figured; he 'enunciated the alphabet and recited the Book of Souls'.[4]

[1] That is, as archetype of a dying person about to enter the higher life, he receives the sacrament of the 'Letter'.

[2] In Semitic folklore, revival from death, deep sleep, or a swoon is accompanied by a sneeze. See below, p. 35.

[3] The vast dimensions of cosmic Adam appear, not only in gnostic texts, but also in Rabbinic literature. The Adam of the Naaseni (Hippolytus, *Refutation of all Heresies*, bk. v, ii, A-N Library, vol. i, p. 130) was 'like that of the Chaldaeans', a 'huge image of Him who is above'. Irenaeus, describing the Ophite doctrine of the unsuccessful creation of an Anthropos by Yaldabaoth, says the figure was of enormous dimensions (Irenaeus, *Ag. Her.*, bk. i, xxx, A-N Library, vol. i, p. 107). The insistence upon vast size helps to identify the angel of gigantic proportions, who appears with a female angel called Holy Spirit to reveal Elkasai's book (Hippolytus, op. cit., bk. ix, viii, A-N Library, vol. i, p. 346) as the androgynous Adam, Adam Kasia.

[4] See p. 19, n. 6.

And he arose and took [*fronds?*] from that Date-palm and made himself a crown and said:

'Thou art the Father, Thou art the Brother and Thou art the Son:[1] Thou art the Offshoot and Thou art the Root of the First Life! Thou art the First and Thou art the Last! Thou, O Date-palm, [*art*] my Father and [*Thou*], Wellspring, my Mother from whom I derive being.'

Then he said 'In the name of the Great Life Who is spirit and soul, health and purity, sealing and armed-readiness! May there be speech and hearing and forgiveness of sins for me, Mara-ḏ-Rabutha—ADAM, son of Hibil-Ziwa, who came into the world as result of mysteries, as result of purification of the soul. For I have cleansed the mysteries of the Body.' . . . (*ATŠ*, pp. 118 ff.)

The second paragraph starts with 'In the name of the Great Life', a formula which precedes every sacred utterance in the sacred books. Adam throughout is the archetype of spiritual humanity and priesthood, of Adam as crowned and anointed Mankind.

The cosmic Body, the *'ṣṭuna* in which Adam Qadmaia appears in *ATŠ* and other texts, includes the worlds of light and the worlds of darkness. Man's body has organs and parts which perform what are thought to be menial functions and the cosmic Body of Adam, although immaterial inasmuch as it is the ideal counterpart of the universe, likewise possesses organs of digestion and evacuation: they are realms assigned to spirits of darkness and pollution, but also of catharsis. Thus:

. . . and so, when food goes down and reaches the inside, the lower belly, Šdum-Daiwa [*a being of the underworlds*] cometh and by his agency and strength bringeth the excrements forth by way of Karafiun and two worlds, so that they come and fall into Ṣihiun (Sion),[2] a valley which is the dumping-ground of dung and urine in one place. It is the world below the Ocean. . . . (*ATŠ*, p. 163.)

So, too, the 'nobler' parts of man are assigned to the great spirits of light and life, or worlds of light:

[1] Cf. a passage in the John Apokryphon quoted by Quispel, *Gnosis als Weltreligion*, p. 14: 'I am the Father, I am the Mother, I am the Son, I am the Eternally Existent, the Unmixed who mingled Himself with Himself.'

[2] This is probably an allusion to Jerusalem, with its Dung-Gate, and the valley into which refuse was cast.

... and to each of them their light is mutually visible, pleasing and displayed: their rays are formed like one another for they are all of light: all form part of the single Body. And each of them is a world. And if it happened that these worlds divided it would be as if one of them were divided. The Body is One, and one the division.

The head is one world, the breast one world and each leg a world: *yea even* unto liver, spleen, bowels, stomach, male organ, womb, skin, hair, nails, back and viscera, each one of them is a separate world.[1] And when they commune together it is as between persons in whom there is no hatred envy or dissension. And if, amongst all these [worlds] there were one superfluous or another lacking from the structure of the Body, the whole Body would be harmed for they counterpoise one another and the Soul dwelleth in their midst as they with one another. And should they not be counterpoised one would corrupt the other and they, together with Body and Soul, would not be mutually established.

For when the Body formed itself, the Soul was formed, and when the Soul took shape in the Body the Body formed the vital spirit [*ruha*]. And when both had taken shape, the Womb was formed, for the Womb is a great world, there is nothing greater or more powerful than it. (*ATŠ*, 163 ff.)

The Mystic Adam is androgynous, and the male organ represents the Father principle: it distributes (Diwan Malkuta 'laita) 'streams of living water' (i.e. Water of Life), and in *ATŠ* it is said of it:

And the male organ is vigorous in its strength and imperial majesty and the Body, [*that is*] the earth[2] and sky and the worlds of light and darkness, is equipped therewith. It is a strong Implement

[1] This list of correspondences should be compared with that in the *Greater Bundahišn*, where the cosmic body is said to have 'skin like the sky, flesh like the earth, bones like mountains', &c. See *Greater Bundahišn*, 189, 8, quoted by Professor Zaehner in *Zurvan* (p. 145). Similar correspondences between microcosm and macrocosm (bones like rocks, veins like rivers, &c.) appear in two medical treatises by Hippocrates, *De Hebdomadibus*, bk. vi (*Works*, ed. M. P. E. Littré, Paris, 1839–61, vol. ix, p. 436), and *De Diaeta*, bk. iv (ibid., vol. vi, pp. 652 ff.). Their date and origin are uncertain but Oriental influence is to be suspected.

[2] True to the macrocosm-microcosm pattern, the earth too has an anthropomorphic shape, 'the earth is a body, and air the soul therein. Its sproutings are bones, rivers veins, blood the ocean . . .', &c. (*ATŠ*, p. 165, No. 223.)

and *malkuta* (kingliness) resembleth it.... For seven kings[1] are incorporated therein standing in seven garments and written with seven letters, namely G A B A R U T A [virility]. (*ATŠ*, p. 166.)

In *ARZ* the organ of virility is assigned to 'Abathur of the Scales', the celestial being who weighs souls after death in his balances against the soul of Seth, and semen is attributed to Hibil-Ziwa 'because thou, Hibil-Ziwa, art the Living Seed: Thou rulest us and all worlds.' This scroll also assigns the bowels, spleen, and liver (lines 177 ff.) to the rulers of the underworld, such as 'the great Giu' and 'the great Gaf', and so on.

In Diwan Malkuta 'laita and *ARZ* the identification and naming of the organs and parts of the body (i.e. spiritual Body, both of the departed soul and of Adam Kasia) are connected with the recitation of liturgical prayers, as the latter mark the gradual formation of the spiritual body for the deceased during the celebration of the *masiqta*. In *ARZ* these prayers are said 'in praise of and obeisance to' the various organs and limbs named.

When thou recitest the major 'Blessed and praised is Life'[2] thou renderest praise and makest obeisance to the bowels; and when thou recitest *Ṭab ṭaba lṭabia*,[3] thou offerest praise and makest obeisance to the liver. (*ARZ*, lines 20 ff.)

The priest belives that during the recitation of prayers and hymns during the *masiqta*, with the loaves and wine-cup before him on his altar-table, these very organs are being formed for the soul of the deceased in the Cosmic Womb, represented by the wine-cup. The body of the embryo in process of formation is not of matter but of its spiritual equivalent.[4] What function were these spiritual organs supposed to perform?[5] As in the

[1] The 'kings' are the seven letters which compose the word, each letter having magic qualities.

[2] *CP* 71.

[3] *CP* 72. 'Good is the good thing [*or* '*Good One*'] for the good.'

[4] The resurrection body of Christ described in St. Luke xxiv. 39 is a material body: 'Handle me and see; for a spirit hath not flesh and bones as ye see me have.'

[5] The same question was rhetorically posed by Tertullian about the resurrection body, see *The Writings of Q. S. F. Tertullianus*, A-N Christian Library (Clarke, Edinburgh, 1869–70, 2 vols), vol. i, pp. 326 ff. His answer

case of the Divine Man, Adam Kasia, the function is that of the gradual purification and elimination of elements of darkness and grossness, incurred during association with the flesh. For the spiritual body must pass through worlds of purification called *maṭarata* before it reaches the worlds of light.[1]

The Body is permeated and held together by light. According to *ATŠ* the blood which circulates in the Body

> . . . is lovely radiance and the Blood which is within the Heart is precious and sublime Radiance. The Blood in its Liver is lovely and plenteous Radiance that moveth in all the Body.
>
> These are four lights which control the Body: had they been three, the Body would not be established. (*ATŠ*, p. 164.)

In the same book the Secret Adam, here called Adam-Shaq (Adam-was-bright) or Adam-Shaq-Ziwa, as Priest, is shown in the character of celebrant of mysteries and Creator.

> And then he planned celebration of the *masiqta*[2] and the *qnasa*[3]

was that although this body had organs of digestion, sexual reproduction, and so on, a change, a 'cessation of office' had taken place.

The gnostics seem to have abandoned completely the Jewish and Persian idea that bones when the dead arise are the seed of a body of flesh and blood. The Zoroastrians, after birds and beasts had picked the skeleton free from polluting decomposing flesh, placed the bones in *astodans*. Oriental Jews have a tradition that the Havdalah meal strengthens a certain bone at the base of the neck which is nourished only by the Sabbatical Havdalah food. When a man dies and his bones moulder, this bone resists decomposition and becomes the seed of a new body at Resurrection. The Rabbinic word for the indestructible bone is לוז (*lūz*), literally an 'almond' or 'nut'. This may explain the presence on the *masiqta* table of nuts (usually walnuts) although these for the Mandaeans have only a symbolic meaning, like seeds also placed on the altar.

Mandaeans are so far from a materialistic view of life after death that graves are neglected and allowed to sink back into the earth after the third day, when the soul is thought to be detached from the corpse and ready to 'arise', only awaiting the formation of its 'light-body', which is necessary before it can leave the earth. On the day of burial the grave is sealed (see *MMII*, p. 186), and on the third day the seal (which wards off evil spirits) is removed.

[1] See *DA*, p. iv. The soul must give a password at each *maṭarta*. Originally planets, in later manuscripts the *maṭarata* are given other names.

[2] The *masiqta* (lit. 'raising-up', 'resurrection') resembles in many features the mass. The bread on the ritual table represents the dead, and during the rite, seeds and nuts and a tiny fragment of the dove's flesh are placed on the wafers. Celebration of the *masiqta* is fully described in *WW*, pp. 242–5.

[3] The *qnasa* of the dove follows the milling and pounding rites described on the next page. See *WW*, pp. 247 f.

[propitiatory rite] of mysteries. And he brought wheat with mysteries and celebrated the *masiqta* of 'Hibil and his Brethren'.[1]

And he stripped and robed, then submerged himself with 360 submersions and sealed himself with 360 names. He submerged himself seven times, [*and then* ?] was baptized with the baptism of 'Hibil-Ziwa and his brethren'.

And he raised himself up, Adam-Shaq-Ziwa, and thus did he constitute his Body ['*ṣṭuna*] and all the mysteries were established.

And the Body took shape, shone, was effulgent of Itself, and gave forth light.

And he remained alone for a thousand thousand years, an endless [*time*] until living Seed went forth and mysteries became hot and assembled in the *Kimṣa*.[2]

And he devised and created seven worlds of radiance [*ziwa*] at his right and seven worlds of light [*nhura*] at his left; and created seven worlds of illusion at beholding which the eyes of 'uthras and kings turn aside in awe. (ibid., trs. pp. 227–8.)

The word used for baptism is *maṣbuta* (lit 'immersion') and this first act was performed alone and was a self-baptism. The second demanded con-celebrants.

The word *qnasa* suggests piacular sacrifice, and these 'sacrifices' take place *before* the actual *masiqta*, and correspond closely to the Parsi *Paragna*,[3] for they refer primarily to the milling of the wheat and crushing and pounding together of the sesame and dates. The latter when strained provide the sacred oil of unction, the *miša*.

The *masiqta* itself takes place within the cult-hut (*škinta* or *bimanda*), and it is within this *sanctum sanctorum*, which no layman enters, that the ceremonies which represent according to

[1] This is the purifying *masiqta*, or rather the 360 *masiqtas*, which were necessary to cleanse Hibil-Ziwa and the spirits who accompanied him on their return from the worlds of darkness (see pp. 56 ff.).

[2] Untranslatable. Lidzbarski described it as a word of cosmic significance. Occasionally, as here, the context suggests a place where a process of perfection is taking place, a womb. Elsewhere, 'climax', 'consummation', appears to be an approximate meaning.

[3] The *haoma* in the *Paragna* rite is pounded in a mortar (like the dates and sesame in the Mandaean preparation for the *masiqta*) and strained in a strainer: the Mandaeans strain the sesame and date juice through a white cloth. See *WW*, pp. 202 ff.

the secret commentaries the sacramental formation of the light-body, in and through Adam Kasia, now called Adakas Ziwa, take place. We shall return to it in a later chapter.

Note. Blood-sacrifice was condemned by the Essenes and, apparently, by all the baptizing Jewish and Jewish-Christian sects baptism was considered to have replaced sacrifice. 'The sacrificial system', says W. D. Davies in *Paul and Rabbinic Judaism* (S.P.C.K. 1955), p. 254, 'was not fully satisfactory to the religious sensibilities of first-century Pharisaic Judaism'. When the destruction of the Temple made blood-sacrifice in the Temple no longer possible, something had to take its place. H. J. Schoeps in *Theologie u. Geschichte des Judenchristentums* (Tübingen, 1949), p. 225, reminds us that the distaste for the sacrifice of animals was no new thing in the first century: it went back to the prophets and 'Schon die Essäer scheinen in ebionitischer Weise die Tieropfer des jerusalemer Tempelkults mit eigenen Weihen (heilige Bäder und Waschungen) ersetzt zu haben)'.

Amongst Mandaeans there is an oral tradition that some of them were once vegetarians. As they are, above all things, baptizers, the sacrifice of the dove is out of the picture entirely. Its slaughter is unmentioned in the *GR* or in the liturgy and its silent killing before the *masiqta* and the tiny gobbet of its flesh placed with the ritual fruit and nuts on the *faṭiria*, like the tradition that it is called the *ba*, are inexplicable.

There are pictures of the dove and of a lamb on a ritual table in an illustrated *šarḥ* describing the Blessed Oblation. The yearly slaughter of a male lamb at Parwanaiia,[1] which usually takes place before the *masiqta*, but not always in the sacred enclosure, has nothing whatever to do with the latter sacrament, although a small piece of the fat is placed later on the Blessed Oblation table. The slaughter (with the usual formula for slaughter of a bird or beast) takes place on the fifth day of the feast. It appears to be nothing more or less than the yearly slaughter of a male lamb practised by a number of religious bodies all over the Middle East (e.g. the Yazidis) and regarded as a spring custom.

The formula whispered voicelessly by the priest who slaughters the dove, in a specially washed and segregated square in the sacred enclosure, has a slight addition, for the priest tells it that it will rise with the commemorated souls.

[1] The lamb is paid for by the community, and its flesh later cut up and distributed amongst the housewives of the village. It is eaten by the various families who contributed to its cost.

The word 'sacrifice' attached to the milling and pounding of grain and fruit is unmentioned in canonical exoteric texts. There is no hint of sacrifice in the commentaries or liturgical prayers which relate to the *masiqta* rites within the *bimanda*.

Of the nature of propitiatory rites and 'ransoms' generally in the Middle East, I wrote in *WW*, chap. ix.

IV

ADAM AND HIS SONS

As already said at the beginning of the last chapter, the Secret Adam is also the archetype of Adam the pattern of a human being who, wedded to Hawa (Eve), is father to mankind. This Adam represents human nature with all its aspirations, failings, and follies, and admonitions to Adam abound in such books as the *GR*. His selfishness is the theme of an allegorical story, a *hieros-logos*, told in that book. He has reached the patriarchal age of a thousand years when word is brought by celestial messengers that his time to depart the body has come. Adam is unpleasantly surprised for he has no wish to leave the world: he wants to live for another thousand years. 'Go', says he, 'to my son Šitil (Seth) and summon him in my stead, for he is well fitted for the other world, since he has had nothing to do with women, has never shed blood and in all his eighty years has led a pure life.' The messengers return to the Great Life and report. Adam's suggestion is accepted by Divine Will and the messengers go again to earth. Visiting Seth the Pure, they summon him to leave the body. Seth, surprised, says that his father, far older than himself, has precedence, and asks whether it would not be better that Adam should quit the earth before senility came upon him or disappointment in his offspring. 'Besides,' he adds modestly, 'I have done no mighty works.' The messengers explain that Adam is loath to leave the world and has sent them to him. Seth engages in prayer, joyfully lays aside his body of flesh and blood, and puts on the dress of glory and light.

It is this act of filial devotion, say the priests, which makes Seth the purest of all human souls, against whose self-sacrifice and virtue souls must be weighed in the scales of judgement. If a departed soul is pure enough to counterpoise the soul of Seth, Abathur permits it to pass on from the judgement seat to Mšunia Kušṭa.[1] If not, it must return to the *maṭarata*[2] for further purgation.

There are several contradictory accounts of Adam's creation. In *GR*r 13: 9 there is the bare statement

Adam the Man and Hawa his wife were formed and the soul [*nišimta*] fell into the body. And when the soul fell into the body, they discerned and understood all things.

The statement is repeated in the same book and with it the corollary that 'angels of fire' served him. In *GR*r 101–2 the unsuccessful creation of Adam by Pthahil is related, and that the imperfect and lifeless creature[3] was completed by Adakas-Mana who added a soul. In *GR*r 172: 13 it is Yawar-Ziwa who comes to the rescue and places the soul in the inert body made by Pthahil, and in another account of Pthahil's vain attempt, it is Pthahil himself who, aghast at his inability to breathe life into Adam's body, appeals to his father, Abathur, with whose help a *mana kasia* (occult *mana*) is procured from the House of Life and placed in the bodies of the human pair. Thereupon Adam sneezed[4] and came to life. It was unwillingly that the soul came from the House of Life (*GR*l 74: 18) and before she entered Adam's body she lamented and wept.

The metaphysical Adam appears in the *GR* and other canonical books under another name, Adakas (a contraction of Adam-Kasia) or Adakas-Ziwa, the Light-Adam. Adakas is the metaphysical Adam, the wholly spiritual humanity. He is the macrocosm conceived not only as an Idea but as an Ideal. Adakas is Adam the microcosm's guardian, his soul, his *mana*, a messenger sent to him, a 'youthful boy',[5] and in *GR*r 245: 13 ff. Adakas-Mana proclaims himself to be

[1] See Chapter V.

[2] Places-of-detention (customs-houses), at the frontiers of worlds through which the soul must pass and expiate her evil deeds and impurities. See p. 30, n. 1.

[3] Variations of the myth such as unsuccessful creation as a prone lifeless figure, usually of huge shape, constantly appear in gnostic, Rabbinic, and Kabbalistic writings.

[4] Like his prototype, see p. 26.

[5] Petermann's text (pp. 235–6) and Lidzbarski's translation (pp. 236–7) give many of these aspects in a haggadic form.

the Head, Adakas the occult *mana* who came from Its place. Our name is 'Offspring', the 'World of Law' they call me. Our name is Resurrection of Life, our name is Tanna, our name is 'living flames'. And I, my name is secret: it came from the House of Life. I am Adakas, the Radiance which came from the Secret Place.

He is also the Word (*GR*r 235: 17 and *GR*r 236) who comes from the great mighty Mana's presence.

Adakas-Ziwa's spouse, Anana-Ziwa,[1] also called Hawa-Kasia (Occult Breath or Pneuma-Eve), produces three pairs of twins, male and female (*GR*r 104), to whom names symbolic of life and light are given. Finally the triad Hibil (Abel), Šitil (Seth), and Anuš (Enos) are born.

Hibil, usually Hibil-Ziwa, is the light-bearer; his other names are Hibil-Yawar (the dazzling Hibil), Hibil-Mana, and Hibil-'uthra. He is essentially a saviour-spirit: it is he who descends to the dark underworld to free souls imprisoned there and to bring back with him from the great 'Well of Darkness' the *gimra* (pearl), i.e. the soul, and a mysterious *mrara*[2] (bitterness)—can it be the bitterness destined to be the lot of the soul on earth? How he achieves his ends is told in more than one version; and the purifying rites necessary before he could be readmitted to celestial circles described in priestly scrolls serve as patterns for those which must be gone through on earth for seriously polluted persons. (*MdHZ.*)

Šitil (Seth)[3]—*Šitil ṭaba*, 'the good plant'—appears as the genius of the human soul, the archetype of a spiritually perfect human personality, sometimes as religion itself. It is Šitil who meets 'souls' on their way to baptism (*ML*, p. 31, No. 21) and teaches them that the true witnesses to the sacrament are not, as they

[1] 'Cloud-of-Radiance'. *Anana* or *anan* (cloud) = 'spouse'—of celestial beings (also of priests!).

[2] Lidzbarski suggested 'bitter herb'. *MdHZ* adds a mirror.

[3] Šitil (Seth). In the OT, Gen. iv. 25, שֵׁת was the third son of Adam. The verb שִׁית means 'to place', 'set', 'put'. The three-letter root ŠTL. (שְׁתַל) means 'to transplant'. It was from the latter Aramaic root with its enriched meaning that Naṣoraeans derived their name for Seth, for Šitil is the transplanted soul or *mana*. The forty-eight or more Coptic MSS. found at Naga Hammadi in 1946 apparently honour Seth as just this.

first suggest, Sun, Moon, or Fire, but the Jordan, *pihta* (sacramental bread), *kušṭa* (the ritual handshake symbolical of good faith and sincerity), *mambuga* (sacramental drink), the Blessed Oblation, and the sanctuary itself.

Anuš (Enos in the Authorized version of the OT—the word like Adam means 'mankind') is patron and promoter of Naṣirutha—and of Naṣoraeans who profess and practise it. He is active as healer and guide:

I took upon me a bodily form and went to the place Jerusalem; I spoke with my voice and preached, I became a Healer to Miriai . . . I was a healer of *kušṭa* [i.e. a true healer] who cureth and taketh no fee. I took Miriai[1] down into the Jordan and baptized her and signed her with the pure sign. (*GR*r 332: 1 ff.)

In the *Haran Gawaita* Anuš guides the persecuted Naṣoraeans to Harran and later into Babylonia, and he avenges them by destroying Jerusalem.

In the same manuscript Anuš or Anuš-'uthra as he is also called, as patron of Naṣirutha protects, baptizes, educates, and initiates John the Baptist. In both *GR* and Drašia ḏ-Yahia he appears as intercessor for his clients, the Naṣoraeans.

Returning to Adakas-Ziwa, the Secret Adam, as over-soul of humanity, he 'fell into Adam' and Eve, the parents of mankind, after twins had been born to them (*GR*r 243 ff.).

He raised them to their feet, lightened their eyes so that they saw, established their feet for going forward, opened their mouths for eating and placed Adam as ruler over animals, fruit, grapes, trees and the winged birds and fish in the sea which his father Pthahil[2] had provided for Adam when planning for him.

[1] A converted Jewess; see *JB* and *ML* under Mirjai.

[2] In the *GR* and other Mandaean texts there is much reference to Pthahil as an unsuccessful creator, but in the secret scrolls he hardly appears at all and there are only a few brief references to his name. In the Canonical Prayers he is mentioned four times but not as a creator. In the cycle of gnostic poems entitled 'When the Pure, Chosen One went', which describe creation, three long poems of the series refer to him as disgraced (by his failure as creator). These three poems are omitted from *CP*. They deal with his punishment and eventual reinstatement. The first two of the three are included in *GR*r 342 ff., but the third is omitted in some copies (as in Petermann's facsimile). This might indicate that Pthahil's failure to place the

In the same context (*GR*r 244: 14) Adakas claims to be chief of all mysteries, protector of the race of mankind over the earth, guardian of the human foetus in the womb of human mothers, and president over its birth. In short Adakas is the guardian-spirit, the *dmuta*, the Over-soul of the human race, of all the descendants of Adam Pagria—his small reflection on the material earth.

Adam Pagria, the microcosm, and his three sons Hibil, Šitil, and Anuš have nothing in common with the Jewish myth of Adam and his sons and grandson but their names, nor do the three brothers belong to the world of earthly mankind. But they preside at baptism and enter into most human activities as promoters and guardians. They are constantly mentioned and invoked in Mandaean literature.

breath of life in his creature Adam, which contradicts other stories of man's creation in the *GR*, was not accepted as part of the original gnosis. He is constantly mentioned in *GR*, and in Drašia ḏ-Yahia the unsuccessful creation story is prominent. In the Ophite story of Yaldabaoth's failure to make man in his own image, Prounikos, the Mother, comes to his aid (Irenaeus, *Ag. Her.*, bk. i, xxx, A-N Library, vol. i, p. 107). Lidzbarski (*JB* xxvii) suggested a connexion between Pthahil and the Egyptian god Ptaḥ. Should this be so, such a connexion may point to an adoption through Alexandrian circles of Ptaḥ into the Creation story as Pthahil. Both R. Reitzenstein (*Poimandres. Studien zur griechisch-ägyptischen und frühchristlichen Literatur* (Leipzig, 1904), p. 248) and A. Festugière (*La Révélation d'Hermès Trismégiste*, vol. i, p. 81) mention a Hermetic confraternity which flourished between the second century B.C. and second century A.D., even reaching Rome. The founder of the sect was an Egyptian priest who combined the doctrine of creation of the world by Ptaḥ with an Oriental revelation about the enslavement and redemption of man. 'Avec le temps, la doctrine revêt un aspect de plus en plus mystique et l'élément égyptien y tient plus de place. . . . Au IVe siècle, la confrérie disparaît à nos yeux.'

V

MŠUNIA KUŠṬA: THE WORLD OF IDEAL COUNTERPARTS

MŠUNIA KUSṬA[1] is an ideal world, one removed from this world: it is a world of true being, a supra-mundane world of ideas, in which is found the double, the counterpart, of everything in the material world. It is the home of Anuš אנוש (*Anuš-'utra*), to which he returned after his bodily appearance in Jerusalem, for he

> . . . came and walked in Jerusalem when he had put on a robe of water-clouds, in bodily semblance. He was not clothed in a physical garment: there was no heat or perturbation in him. He went and came in the years of Pilate [Palṭus], a worldly king.
>
> Anuš-'uthra came to the world in the strength of the great King of Light, healing the sick, opening the eyes of the blind, cleansing the leprous, raising up the broken and those who shuffle on the ground to walk on their feet, making the deaf and dumb to speak, the dead to live and gaining believers amongst the Jews and showing them that 'there is death and there is life: there is darkness and there is light. There is error and there is truth' and converting Jews in the name of the High King of Light.
>
> Three hundred and sixty prophets emigrate from the town of Jerusalem testifying to the name of Mara-ḏ-Rabutha.
>
> And Anuš-'uthra mounteth upward and remaineth in Mšunia-Kušṭa. (*GR*r 29.)

The story is probably a polemic against Christianity in which the miracles of Jesus are attributed to Anuš, who, according to

[1] The expression is difficult to translate. *Mšunia* is a West-Aramaic form (see *JB*, p. xvii): it is derived from the root ŠNA, not in the sense 'to remove', as Lidzbarski thought, but in the second root-meaning, related to TNA, 'to double', 'repeat'. *Kušṭa* ('truth', 'verity', &c.) has here the extended meaning of 'reality', for it is the ideal counterpart which is real, not its reflection in matter.

Mandaeans, was a 'son of Man', that is of Adam Kasia, himself a counterpart (*dmut*) and Son of the supreme Being.

Mšunia Kušṭa must be translated by a paraphrase: it is a sublime other-world of reality, for this material world is illusion, unreal, temporary.

In my book *MMII* I gave an account of this world as given to me by Mandaeans in 'Iraq:

> Mšunia Kušṭa is the ideal world of the Mandaeans and peopled by the descendants of Adam-Kasia and Hawa-Kasia [the hidden or mystical Adam and Eve]; for, as one priest told me, 'of all things there are two, an actual and its *mabda* [ideal or archetype]'. Another explained that each individual on earth has his double [*dmuta*] or likeness in Mšunia Kušṭa and at the time of death the earthly individual leaves his earthly body and assumes the ethereal body of his double. (*MMII*, pp. 54–55).

Part of that explanation, namely the last clause, could be modified by the 'Adam' teaching which will be dealt with later. The theory of doubles is Iranian as well as Platonic. Sir J. J. Modi writes:[1]

> On the death of a person, his soul [*urvân* or *ravân*] meets with justice according to his merits or demerits. If he has deserved well he goes to heaven, if not to hell. His Fravashi, which guided him through life as a guiding spirit, parts from his soul and goes to its abode or place among all the Fravashis. It is the soul [*urvân*] that meets with good or evil consequences of its actions. The Fravashi or the guiding spirit, was pure and perfect, unalloyed and uncontaminated from the beginning and has passed away as such. So it is this pure and spiritual identity, the Fravashi, that is the medium, as it were, of the continued relation between the living and the dead.

Modi goes on to say that, according to the Avesta, all natural objects have their Fravashis, but not objects that have been made from those natural objects:

> For example, the trees have their Fravashis, but not the chair or table that has been made from the wood of the tree. God has created

[1] J. J. Modi, *The Religious Ceremonies and Customs of the Parsees* (British India Press, Bombay, 1922), p. 423.

the Fravashis of these natural objects from the very beginning of creation. Before the creation of the object, there existed the Fravashi of that object, perfect, complete and correct.

The Fravardin Yašt, which is in praise of the Fravashis, seems to dwell chiefly on their office as guardian spirits. Their presence in the material world is necessary to the struggle with Ahriman and evil, so they hover everywhere as protectors of men, trees, sun, moon, cattle, and all the good creations of Ahura-Mazda, guarding, warning, and blessing. In the Bundahišn Ohrmazd (the Pahlavi version of Ahura-Mazda) appeals to the fravahrs (Pahlavi form of Fravashi) of human beings and invokes their aid. At death the fravahr separates itself from the body (*tanu* or *asta* = 'bones')[1] and rejoins its fellow guardian spirits.

Plato's ideal world is akin to both the Mandaean Mšunia Kušṭa and the Parsi world of prototypes:

The temperature of their seasons is such that they are free from disease and live much longer than we do; and in sight and hearing and smell and the other senses they are as much more perfect than we as air is purer than water and ether than air. Moreover they have sanctuaries and temples of the gods, in which the gods dwell in very truth. (*Phaedo* 111 b.)

The air of Mšunia Kušṭa, too, is etheric, and worship there is perpetual, the archetype of earthly worship.

Mšunia Kušṭa is reached after purification, and is not the final goal.[2]

And thus, as they depart, set forth and fly into the sky, traversing the road, they behold the Gate of Mercies which is opened in the midst of Mšunia Kušṭa and then they move onwards and sit at the boundary that bounds Mšunia Kušṭa which no earthly being may cross unless signed with the sign of the Jordan in true sincerity [*lit. and kušṭa was therein*]. So there spirit and soul wait until they are taken up into worlds of light.

And from the day that she departeth [*the body*] till the day that she setteth forth, she [*the soul*] beholdeth those forms, trees and souls

[1] See p. 29, n. 4.

[2] In the *Phaedo* 114 c the spirits of the holy departed 'go to dwellings still fairer than these'.

which exist upon Mšunia Kušṭa. If she hath taken a 'Letter of oil' [1] she will [*traverse*] the sixty parasangs from that Gate in forty-five days.

And in that place at each stretch of the way there is a gate through which souls must pass. If the soul be a good one, the gates are opened in a single day and a glorious light appeareth from the beginning of the road unto the last of the gates of Mšunia Kušṭa. She beholdeth them in light and effulgence and knoweth not whither she is going until she cometh out of that place, departeth by that gate [*leaving behind*?] the torment of existence.

And so, as she departeth from that place, she will assume a beauteous appearance and will be in fair raiment. And when she putteth on that raiment she will remain therein.

And there are dwellings therein for it is called the Dwelling of Abathur: it is the place in which souls are kept until they depart therefrom.

And all souls which we have brought thither drink of yon Jordan and pluck and eat of yon tree. And they go about freely: in those worlds there is no sighing[2] because the soul's body in that world resembleth trees which drink of wind and water and live. They partake of the fruit but there is no excrement amongst them, neither is there any consuming flame or fire with them which blazeth. When they cast incense, their radiance shines out, and it wreathes up before them. And when they wish to make *pihta*[3] they divide the wheat from the ear and thus make [*bread*].

And those who brought them into the celestial worlds open walnuts and quince and make the *pihta* with all the *ginzia*.[4]

None of the trees that grow there have pip or seed in them and (yet) their fruit neither diminishes nor is it of poor quality. (*ATŠ*, pp. 189–90.)[5]

The writer of *ATŠ* describes how Hibil-Ziwa, when baptizing Adam and Eve, procured bread (*pihta*), sacramental drink (*mambuha*), myrtle, and incense from Mšunia Kušṭa.

[1] The 'Letter' is the rite for the dying (see p. 73).

[2] *Tinta* also means 'urination' (as it may here, as a word-play).

[3] The sacramental bread. The meaning is, that there it needs no baking.

[4] i.e. all the fruits, nuts, and other necessary adjuncts for the sacramental meal.

[5] A similar ideal world is described in the Parthian Manichaean hymns (see *The Manichaean Hymn-Cycle in Parthian* translated by Dr. Mary Boyce: the *Huwīdagmān*, i, pp. 67–77.

Because souls clothed with an [earthly] body neither consume nor perceive food and drink which is from above, [from] Mšunia Kušṭa; and bodies which (exist) on Mšunia Kušṭa do not eat of food of the Second [*i.e. material*] world on account of the mysteries of death which are inherent therein. Any person who eateth earthly food but wisheth to depart the body should [consume] nothing but that of the *masiqta*, the 'Letter', the Commemoration and the 'Of the Fathers and forgiving of souls',[1] for they [*sacramental foods*] rise hence and are given to souls.[2] (Ibid., pp. 190–1 trs.)

That this over-soul or spiritual counterpart acts as guardian spirit appears here and there in Mandaic stories, as for example when Miriai, the Jewish princess converted to Naṣirutha, falls asleep in the *bit maškna* (sanctuary). Her fellow worshippers slip out without awakening her, but her 'sister in Kušṭa' rouses her and bids her wake and depart before cockcrow. Occasionally the soul itself is called a 'sister in Kušṭa' as in *ATŠ*, p. 241, and later, in the same scroll, the *dmut* or *dmuta* appears as conscience:

Amongst [*them are*] those whose feet stumbled and whose *dmuta* warned them so that they perceived her and knew. Such men are elect and redeemed Naṣoraeans. (Ibid., p. 363.)

Dmuthiia (Counterpart-of-Life) is the name of one of the divine male and female twins born to the mystic Adam and Eve (see p. 36), her twin being 'Son-of-Life'. Of her it is said 'from her (Dmuthiia) the world was called into being'. If the passage is continued without a stop, she appears as the mother of Hibil, Šitil, and Anuš, instead of, or as a counterpart of, Eve (Hawa). She, or he, for the sex varies, is often praised, worshipped, and identified with other emanations of the Great Life. In his preface to *Tafsir Pagra* (part ii of *ATŠ*, p. 168) the priestly author writes of his treatise:

And the Aspect [*Parṣufa*] of Mara-ḏ-Rabutha [the Lord of Greatness] is portrayed herein. It dissecteth all mysteries and explaineth

[1] Ritual meals commemorating the dead. *Lofani.*

[2] The aged sometimes end their lives voluntarily by eating and drinking nothing but the sacraments. In this way they ensure an easy passage to the worlds of light. I knew of such a case, an old man who after baptism at Panja took no food but *pihta* and no drink but *mambuha* and so died a *šalmana*, a 'perfect'.

about them and it setteth up a lofty explanation about this mystery. And from it emerged an ideal [*dmut*] of life [*hiia*] for, although worlds and generations call it *Dmuthiia*, they do not understand what they are saying, since *Hiia* (Life, Living Ones) meaneth our Parents [*abahatan*], and their *dmut* is this mystery of Naṣirutha which is the expression thereof. (*ATŠ*, p. 168.)

The image of the mirror is employed again and again in this poetical religion. Water mirrors light; one being reflects or is the image of another. To the mystic the reality is not the reflection but the Reflecter, not the material but the Immaterial.

On the day that Radiance became manifest
And emerged from the Inner Radiance,
A counterpart [*dmuta*] of the Jordan formed itself
In its mirror.
And in the Ether water was produced
And water in the Ether was shed abroad:
Shed abroad were the waters in the Ether
And the power of Light divulged itself.
It expressed itself, increased and multiplied.
And the Crown was established and the Wreath twined.
Twined was the Wreath and the leaves of myrtle flourished:
They flourished, the leaves of myrtle
And trees bore their burden [*of fruit*].[1]
Naṣirutha spoke in them and twined their purities
Upon kings from the Beginning to the End. (*ATŠ*, p. 167.)

The world of archetypes as a religious conception reappears in medieval Germany, and Modi's description of the fravahrs quoted earlier in this chapter (see p. 40 f.) agrees with startling accuracy with a description of the archetypal world given by the Jewish mystic Eleazar ben Yehudah of Worms who died at the end of the thirteenth century. He, like the Ḥasidim of Palestine appears, Professor Scholem remarks, to have been influenced by neo-Platonic thought. (May not Jewish Kabbalists have preserved something of the gnosticism of earlier centuries?) I will quote what Professor Scholem says:

Of special interest in this connection is the doctrine of the arche-

[1] 'Trees' and 'vines' usually mean 'believers, those of the true faith'.

types. . . which dominates Eleazar's work on 'The Science of the Soul' but is of importance also for the 'Book of the Devout'. According to this doctrine, every lower form of existence, including lifeless things,—'even the wood block' to say nothing of even lower forms of life—has its archetype, *demuth*. (Scholem, op. cit., p. 117.)

If, with Scholem, we assume that thirteenth-century Jews borrowed conceptions such as these from neo-Platonic writings, it will also be asked at what period did the idea of archetypes penetrate Mandaean–Naṣoraean teaching? Could it not possibly have been introduced during the Moslem period, together with passages which resemble the Hermetica? (see Appendix).

The answer is emphatically No. The entire theology of Naṣirutha rests upon the twin motifs of archetypes and syzygies. This dualism, possibly Magian in origin, perhaps Pythagorean, must have been well rooted in Judaea in the first Christian centuries. We find it in the *Clementine Homilies*, though in a form which seems to suggest that it was part of secret teaching. Thus:

Homily II, chap. XV:[1]

Hence therefore God, teaching men with respect to the truth of existing things, being Himself One, has distinguished all principles into *pairs and opposites*, Himself being sole God from the beginning,

[1] See Carl Schmidt's *Studien zu den Pseudo-Clementinen*, Texte u. Untersuchen zur Geschichte der Altchristlichen Literatur, Band XLVI (Leipzig, 1929), pp. 25 ff. The Ebionite character of the fictionized disputations between Peter and Simon the Magian is apparent; more than that it would be controversial to assert. Hans Waitz, *Die Pseudoklementinen* (Leipzig, 1904), p. 1, H. J. Schoeps, *Theologie u. Geschichte des Judenchristentums*, Texte u. Untersuchungen zur Geschichte der altchristlichen Literatur, Band XXV, and the Tübingen School generally, stress the importance of the Clementines for study of early Jewish-Christianity. Their conclusions have been disputed with some heat by other theologians, e.g. Bultmann in *Gnomon*, xxvi, 1954, p. 177, and with greater reserve by A. D. Nock, *Gnomon*, xxviii, 1956, pp. 621 ff.

The *Clementine Homilies* and *Recognitions* are, according to most scholars, probably based on a lost work (or on lost works) in circulation at the time, called the *Periodoi Petrou* and *Kerygmata Petrou*. The supposed date of these and of the Clementines has been much in dispute. The sources were thought by Schoeps to be dated *circa* A.D. 160–90. Catholic theologians place the *Grundschrift* (original source or sources) somewhere in the first thirty years of the fourth century. A. D. Nock somewhere refers to the whole question as a Sargasso Sea! My own interest in the *Homilies* is, of course, confined to similarities found in them to the secret teaching of the Naṣoraeans.

having made heaven and earth, day and night, light and fire, sun and moon, life and death . . . for since the present *world is Female* . . . but *the world to come is Male*. . . .

Homily II. xvi:

God, who is One, made the heavens first and then the earth like *a right hand and a left*, so likewise did He constitute *all the combinations in order*. . . .

Homily II. xxxiii:

We see all things in *pairs and contraries*.

Homily III. xxxiii:

He, alone . . . made of the *four*[1] *contrary elements* . . . myriads of compounds that, being turned into *opposite natures and mingled*, they might effect the pleasure of life from the *combinations of contraries*.

In Homily III examples of 'the law of conjunctions' are cited, e.g. Simon Magus and his opponent St. Peter (Simon the Magian is called a disciple of St. John the Baptist). Every 'prophet of the truth' is paired with a prophet in some way opposite: Jesus is paired but opposed by John the Baptist, and so on. Archetypes also appear in the Clementines. As in the 'Elkasaite' book (in which W. Bousset saw a connexion with Mandæism[2]) Adam is the archetype not only of humanity, but of a Christ who was a manifestation of the Son of Man, that is the Divine Man.

As for the possibility that neo-Platonism influenced Naṣoraean gnosis *directly*, and 'directly' should be stressed, why did the Naṣoraeans adopt the word *Mana* for the Creative Mind instead of the Greek νοῦς?

[1] In Homily XIX. xii, 'Peter' says that God produced 'hot, cold, moist and dry opposites' in order to create a 'living being', i.e. the cosmos. Cf. the Denkart, which Zaehner quotes on p. 141 of *Zurvan*. Zaehner remarks: 'Now it seems clear enough that all this is based upon Greek physics and we would therefore expect that the four elements would be compounded from the four natural properties (hot, cold, moist and dry).' In the Mandaean *ATŠ* we read 'no Body can exist that is not born of two mysteries and built up of four mysteries'.

[2] W. Bousset, *Hauptprobleme der Gnosis* (Forschungen zur Religion und Literatur des alten u. neuen Testaments, Hft. 10, 1907).

VI

THE SOUL

THREE words used for 'soul' in Mandaic, *nafš*, *ruha*, and *nišimta*, are derived from Semitic roots which mean 'to breathe'. To these the Iranian word *mana* has been added. The word *nafš* means roughly 'self': it is that which expresses individuality, the person; and is only occasionally used for 'soul'. Persons as people are often referred to as *nišmata*, 'souls', or *almia*, 'worlds'.

The *ruha* is the vital spirit (see p. 6), the seat of desire and lust. Personified, it becomes in the *GR* and *JB* the enemy of the *nišimta* (soul), and in polemical passages, as Ruha-ḏ-Qudša (Holy-Spirit), she is a demon, the ally and mother of the planets. In esoteric writings the polemical Ruha-ḏ-Qudša is not mentioned at all: the *ruha* is sometimes portrayed as a trembling sister to the soul, looking to her as a 'sister in kušṭa' for help, or as repentant and longing for redemption.

The spirit speaketh to the soul saying 'By thy life, by thy life [O] Soul! take me with thee as thy companion! If I did loose persecution upon thee, [yet] do in kindness remember me, for I knew not and understood thee not. Well is it for one who walketh in kindliness, for all that he seeks he shall find. (Diwan Malkuta 'laita, lines 213 ff.)

Again, when the novice-priest has performed his first baptism and places his foot on the Jordan-bank:

The spirit [*ruha*] rises up from the depths of the Body ['*ṣṭuna*] and is embraced by the soul [*nišimta*] who is Šitil [Seth], and she says to her 'Take me with thee as thy companion!' (Ibid., lines 507 f.)

Compare this with another passage in the same manuscript:

And They said to them [*candidates for priesthood*] 'Who is He who formed you and in whose lap were ye nurtured?' And they said 'We were nurtured in the lap of Ruha; but my Father, our Father, shaped us, He whose name is Pure-Ether.' And they said 'We have hated the worlds' children and the bed of the Mother, the Companion before whom no [*companion, spouse*] existed.' And they said 'Accursed be Ruha and anathematized! she who liveth in horrid darkness, sitteth in company with devouring fire and drinketh red waters. She weareth garments of many colours, for she doth not cross the great Sea of the End [*yama ḏ-suf*].[1] Blessed is that man who cast off her dress of many colours and put on the vesture of white silk which clothed us. We have rejoiced in the fragrance of Yawar: we drink here of living waters and are delivered from horrid darkness. Woe to them that loved thee, [Ruha] and do not hold themselves aloof from thy company. Woe to those who loved gold and silver . . . did not turn away from Earth, nor came forth from within their Mother. (Ibid., lines 167 ff.)

Of the *mana* we have already spoken. Twenty-eight hymns in the *Ginza* (*GR*l 38: 18 to *GR*l 74: 1 f. and trs. pp. 452–504) begin with the words

I am a *mana* of the Great Life,
A *mana* of the Mighty Life am I,
A *mana* I am of the Great Life.

The first hymn opens with a bitter lament—'Who hath made me dwell on earth, who hath cast me into the physical body (*'ṣṭun pagria*)[2] which hath no hands or feet and knoweth not how it will walk? It lies there and crawls', for this is the soul's complaint when put into the still imperfect Adam. She is comforted: Manda-ḏ-Hiia, Knowledge of Life, comes in answer to her cry of dismay and urges her to rise and seek her home, return to which is assured her. In hymn after hymn we find first the complaint and cry of the imprisoned *mana* and then consolation and promise. These hymns are probably intended to be read antiphonally, first the cry of the *mana* and then the comforting words, and priests still intone them at the graveside or in the homes of mourners.

A second series follows in *GR* in which the chief theme is

[1] A gnostic metaphor for crossing from the world of matter into that of spirit. *Yama ḏ-Suf* = Sea of Reeds, Red Sea, Sea of the End. See p. 83.
[2] *'ṣṭun*, see pp. 5, n. 2 and 21, n. 1.

that of redemption and glory: 'Depart in peace, Chosen, Pure One!', 'Go, soul, triumphant to the Place of Joy', and 'Come in peace, thou pure Pearl!', and in the second series the word *nišimta* is used oftener than *mana*. All these hymns of the soul voice genuine devotion, moving sorrow, and belief in future life.

In all the holy books hatred and horror of the body[1] are expressed, a hatred hardly logical in a people whose whole literature shows delight in life, flowers, trees, and natural beauty. These, however, are not thought hateful. When the soul left worlds of ether she brought with her as consolation some of the lovely gifts of Life.

When the Soul came from worlds of light and fell into the Body, there came with her some of all the mysteries which exist in the world of light: some of its radiance and light, some of its sincerity, some of its unity, its order, its peacefulness and its honesty; some of all that there is in the realm of light came to bear her company, to delight her, to purify her and surround her so that she may commune with them and that there may be for her that which will aid her against the evils and temptations of the earth.

And the evil spirit [*ruha*] came with her, accompanied by all the mysteries that exist in darkness, and into the body she introduced song, frivolity, dancing, deceit and falsehood, excitement and lust, lying and witchcraft, violence and perversion..... For spirit and soul are distinct from one another and I placed strife between them. (*ATŠ*, trs. pp. 215–16.)

In *ARZ*, the soul's dowry is the

. . . sweet-smelling flowers and herbs, and the trees and the good things which we gave to the soul as her escort when she wishes to go to the house of her father-in-law. For she is Our crowned Bride: I give her to them as a bride but they are stupidly indifferent to her, hating her, detesting her heartily; and [*although*] she gives light to their gloomy abode, sweeps it and cleanses it, her mother-in-law grumbles about the bride.

She hangs up lamps of radiance at night, but they say to her 'Thy

[1] 'Good is the day when I depart from thee, stinking body, and when I am purified from evil deeds!' (Diwan Malkuta 'laita, line 209).

lamp gives out no light!' She sets out delicious fare before them and spreads out for them [*couches*], but they remove that which she spreads out, saying to her 'Fetch water instead'[1] or 'Guard the door from thieves!' wishing to get her out of the house.

And they know not that they will die, perhaps falling asleep on their beds into an everlasting sleep on the spot.

And in their folly they slay the living soul, but before they kill her, they kill themselves unwittingly. Then they know that a body without a soul is speechless and that it is the *mana* which establishes it.

I tell you, my brother 'uthras, that we cannot permit the soul to be held back in gloomy darkness!

If a young husband loveth his wife, she will love him and not desire to see her parents: she cuts herself off from them, forgetting her mother's breasts and the home in which she grew up.

If she is an unwilling bride [*lit.* '*hating bride*'] she will get the better of all her slayers, will be spurred on by the compulsion through which she has passed, making her forget her brothers and parents and remain cut off from security.

Nevertheless, We will see to this our holding (property), so that she may come and dwell with Us. (*ARZ*, lines 227–40.)

It must be remembered that the manuscripts just quoted are intended for priests only, and the extracts given only occur here and there, for over the whole gnosis priestcraft broods with menace of penalties in this world and the next should the hundred and one rules for ritual purity and correct procedure be infringed, wittingly or unwittingly. The future of the soul here and hereafter depends, it would seem, less upon virtuous deeds than upon observance of ritual purity and punctual and meticulous performance of all the rites of the Naṣoraean church. A soul which died a 'polluted death', such as in child-birth, or by fire, accident, attack by a wild beast, or under conditions considered ritually impure, becomes 'the portion of Darkness' (*ATŠ*, trs. p. 225) and is doomed to the *maṭarata* unless the relatives of the deceased pay money for redeeming *masiqtas*. Without either 'Letter' or *masiqta* a departed soul has little chance of escaping torment in the future life, and must long sojourn in

[1] Aramaic מלי (see J. vol. 2, 'complement, replace'). To fetch water is the duty of a female servant.

what are practically purgatories. To die naked or wearing ordinary dress is to die in a state of impurity, hence every year during the five intercalary days (Parwanaiia, Panja), the 'five days of light', many persons commission the Blessed Oblation known as *Ahaba ḏ-Mania* (Giving of Garments). A proxy acts the part of the deceased who died 'improperly clothed' and in the latter's name is baptized, puts on a new ritual dress (*rasta*, the word is Persian), and eats the sacred meal.[1] At this time, too, *masiqtas* are celebrated (for fees) and the names of the departed are read in lists at commemorative *Lofanis*—(the literary name is *laufa*, communion, union) at which bread is broken and eaten ritually and water drunk in the same way.

The *ATŠ* in *Tafsir Pagra*, a composition which must be dated after the introduction of the silk-moth into Persia, gives a picture of life after death in which the *maṭarata* are entirely unmentioned:

We, the Great Life, made all mysteries [*ginzia*] and We freed the soul so that she should not remain encaged [in the body]. That which We brought out from Our midst shall come and return to her place, but not in that appearance in which she went forth from amongst Us. When she cometh hither [to be] with Us, she will not go back.

For when We sent her and placed her in the Body like a grain of mustard-seed, We sent her and placed her and gave her to Hibil-Ziwa and she writhed and twisted in his hand when she felt its warmth.

And so he brought and placed her in heat and cold, casting the seed so that it fell into its garment of heat and cold.

And then she emergeth from the Womb as a chicklet cometh forth from the egg. And the soul liveth and issueth from the interior of evil mysteries so that she meeteth the eye and is seen. (*ATŠ*, trs. p. 188.)

Here the manuscript shows signs of imperfection, for a comparison with the silkworm should begin here, but is missing. The 'leaves' referred to in the continuation are mulberry-leaves or, figuratively, leaves from the tree of Naṣirutha.

So they nurture it upon a diet of leaves. And the trees are planted from a Root which is called silk [*sound?*][2] and beareth fruit and blossom

[1] See *MMII*, pp. 214–22.
[2] A bad pun? *Šraia* = 'silk'; *šarira* = 'sound', 'firm'.

and a mystery of blood and water[1] in which seed and stock are preserved. For its name is [*a*]*tutia gawaita*[2] and the worlds and generations call it *tuta* (= 'mulberry', 'remorse').

So it germinated, grew and became strong beneath the throne of the holy Pthahil. Thus it happened that in a little year, that is forty-five days, I perfected that mystery, that mystery pregnant and sown therein. Hence, from that which seeketh *tuta, tuta* goeth forth. That which is named silk [*-worm*] extracted food for itself.

And the soul, like it, made for herself a sky and earth and formed a body [*'ṣṭuna*] therein, like the cocoon which is formed of silk from the thread which issued from the mouth of the worm. For the speech of the worm is of silk, whereas the speech of the soul is prayer and praise.

And so she [the soul] resembleth the worm with that silk and cocoon; for they call it a 'celestial Egg', because two eggs were formed in mystery.

And the one, that which issued from the mouth [*of the worm*] is of silk. The soul, which was placed in [*the other*] wailed and sobbed until her measure was accomplished. And [after] forty-five days[3] she [or it, the moth] emergeth, forceth a way out by the mouth, departeth and flieth in the sublime ether.

And that seed and mystery in which she had been pent they cast into the earth. And so she mounteth up into the sky and none know whither she [*or it*] goeth.

Thus the soul resembleth this in the body which, like the worm, she formed and inhabited, for, when she desireth to depart from it, she openeth a door for herself [to escape] from the body and goeth forth like a dove.

[*Yea*], thus doth the soul, like it, go forth from the body, opening a door from the body for itself. And those doors burst open and We open its structure for it [else] it could not issue from the door of the body.

For [*on entering the body*] she maketh fast all the doors of the body, closeth the gates, blocketh up the portals, taketh upper and lower seals and therewith she covereth [*sealeth*] her garment.

1 The reference is to the 'sacred union' of the cosmic Father and Mother during *masiqta* rites. See *WW*, chap. v.

2 Read *tuta gawaia* (inner remorse). *Tuta* = (*a*) 'sorrow, remorse', (*b*) 'mulberry-tree'.

3 Periods at which rites for the 'rising' or 'raising-up' of the soul are performed, representing stages of her progress, are performed on the third and forty-fifth day after death (see *MMII*, p. 203, n. 16, and *WW*, pp. 149, 185, 234, 257).

And then a cleft is rent in the body which dwelleth in the midst of worlds and generations. And they loosen the girdle of the chosen one and there, at the first aperture, the first formation, is a knot which is a great boundary placed between Light and Darkness. If the soul crosseth it deliberately downward she becometh the portion of Darkness, and if the spirit [*ruha*] passeth over it upward, she becometh the portion of Light.

And so, when spirit and soul have reached their end together and seek to leave the house of the body, there she—each of them severally—looseneth her own mysteries and [then] they fly hand-in-hand into the sublime ether as one. For, when the *ruha* accompanieth the *nišimta*, the twain become, as it were, a single body, like seed and stock formed by two bodies. As they commingle, rejoicing, a [*single*] form resulteth from them.

And thus, as they depart, set forth and fly into the sky, traversing the road, they behold the Gate of Mercies which is opened in the centre of Mšunia Kušṭa. And they move onward and sit at the boundary which bounds Mšunia Kušṭa which no earthly being may cross unless signed with the sign of the Jordan in true sincerity. So there they wait, spirit and soul, until they are taken up into worlds of light. (Ibid., pp. 188–9.)

Of the final union which lies even beyond the worlds of light there are glimpses, chiefly in the hymns. One of the most beautiful is recited at baptism. It is probably one of the oldest.

In the name of the Life!
What did thy Father do for thee, Soul,
The great day on which thou wast raised up?
"He took me down to the Jordan, planted me
And rose and stood me upon its bank.
He broke[1] and gave me bread [*pihta*]
Blessed[2] the cup and gave me thereof to drink.
He placed me between his knees
And pronounced over me the name of the Mighty [Life].
He passed into the mountain before me.
He cried loudly that I might hear,
That I might hear he cried loudly,
'If there is strength in thee, Soul, come!'

[1] *Pta* (lit. 'opened') = 'broke open, broke apart'.
[2] Lit. 'praised'; i.e. pronounced the Benediction.

'If I climb the mountain I shall fall,
I shall overturn and perish from the world!'
I lifted mine eyes to heaven
And my soul waited upon the House of Life.
I climbed the mountain and fell not.
I came and found the life of my Self."

The question is repeated, and the beginning of the reply is the same, then:

"He passed into the fire before me
And cried loudly that I might hear,
That I might hear he cried aloud,
'If there is strength in thee, Soul, come!'

'If I go into fire, I shall burn,
I shall scorch and perish from the world!'
To heaven I lifted mine eyes
And my soul waited upon the House of Life.
I went into the Fire and burned not,
I came and found the life of my Self."

Again there is repetition of the first nine lines, and:

"He entered the sea before me;
He cried aloud that I might hear,
That I might hear he cried aloud,
'If there is strength in thee, Soul, come!'
'If I go into the sea I shall sink,
I shall be overturned and perish from the world!'

To heaven I lifted mine eyes
And my soul waited upon the House of Life.
I went into the sea and was not drowned,
I came, the life of my Self I found."

Yea, Life! Lo, Life!
Life hath triumphed over this world
And Life is victorious. (Prayer 30, *CP*, p. 24.)

In the *GR* we get a picture of the meeting of the archetype, the *dmut* with the soul on its arrival in Mšunia Kušṭa:

I go forth towards my Counterpart and my Counterpart cometh out toward me,
It fondleth and embraceth me as if I came from prison.
(*GR*l 113: 11 f.)

And of the ultimate reunion:

Life supported Life
Life found Its Own
Its Own did Life find
And my soul[1] found
That for which it had yearned.
(*GR*l 90: 10 f. and 101: 17 f.)

The Diwan Malkuta 'laita says (lines 691 ff.):

'Behold! this is the Pearl which came and gave them light! She it is who maketh your stink fragrant. If ye do not desire her, she will not remain with you!'

Then Ayar (Ether) took down the veil which he had drawn over her before them, and when he had taken it down the radiance of the soul shone out over them: they all fell on their faces and said 'Have mercy on us! In her presence we are slaves and we will serve her.'

And when he said

'The Place of Safe-keeping
Which is set apart for the company of the Great [*Life*],'

they all rose to their feet. And as they grasped Ayar's hand in covenant [*kušṭa*] he said

'The Great Life hath stretched forth His right hand to thee!
Put away passion from thy thought!
Thy thought shall be filled with Ours
And thy garment and our Garment shall be one.'

The word 'garment' here means *mana*, so that the last line translated from gnostic cryptogram would read:

And thy *mana* and Our *Mana* shall be one.

That is to say, the soul has reached the Self.

[1] The name of the person for whom the *masiqta* is celebrated should be inserted here.

VII

PERSONIFIED EMANATIONS AND 'UTHRAS

THE ether-world is peopled by angelic beings called 'uthras. The word is derived from a root meaning 'to increase, be abounding'. They become denizens of the ethereal world from the moment that it was called into existence. They are not First Emanations, but they were created by them, although this is often apparently contradicted by what is said of them in the texts. *Malkia*, 'kings', apart from its literal and derived meaning when applied to priests, is a term which may indicate evil beings as well as good: there is a *malka ḏ-nhura* (king of light) and a *malka ḏ-hšuka* (king of darkness), but these are epithets, descriptive of characteristics rather than names of beings. The word *gabra*, 'man', applied to any non-material being does not mean a human being, but a being anthropomorphically visualized; whenever the term *gabra* is applied to such a being in Mandaean literature it must be understood in this way. Myths attached to such beings are usually told in allegorical or folk-tale form, for they are intended for the edification of those not versed in the inner meanings of such parables. In the secret texts there is little, or only remote, allusion to such myths, with the exception of that attached to the saviour-spirit Hibil-Ziwa and his descent into the underworld. Two priestly scrolls make this story the theme upon which to hang an account of the exact way in which a Blessed Oblation and the 'Great Baptism' (360 baptisms) should be celebrated. They are the Šarḥ ḏ-Maṣbuta ḏ-Hibil-Ziwa and the *MḏHZ*. The latter leaves out most of the story as told in the *GR* although the tale is told in a similar lively folk-tale style. Hibil-Ziwa and his companions set out for the underworld in ships, protected by magic talismans, seals, and weapons of holy might, preceded by banners of light to hold spellbound the spirits of darkness who might behold them. The account of the visit to the realms of darkness is brief. Hibil-Ziwa, when he arrives at the world of Anatan and Qin,[1] is welcomed without suspicion. Qin shows her visitor, Hibil-Ziwa, where the jewel (*gimra*), *mrara* (bitterness), and the mirror have been hidden and he pilfers them without her knowledge. He also takes away Ruha who has been mated to her brother and is pregnant of 'Ur and of the 'warriors of Darkness', i.e. the planets. All this is explained in a few short lines: the narrator is chiefly interested in the return and ascent. The first stage of ascent is the 'Letter', which means the sacrament for the dying, in fact the whole sequence of events related represents the rites necessary for the ascension of a soul after death: the ceremonies are described at great length.

The manuscript first mentioned, the Maṣbuta Rabtia, is devoted to a detailed description of the 360 baptisms 'of Hibil-Ziwa' and of the ceremonies and prayers which precede the baptisms, and gives the number of *ganzibria*, priests, *ašgandia*, and banners which must be present. By the time that this text was composed, the number of ecclesiastics had dwindled, so that a method of compressing 360 baptisms into a few had to be contrived. The greater part of the manuscript is devoted to commentary and explanation of all the rites, including the Blessed Oblation and the *Masiqta*.

In the *GR* the story of descent, ascent, and return is told quite delightfully.[2] It is an ancient story, a version of which is related in Apuleius's *Golden Ass* as the story of Eros and Psyche, and part of it may be based on Babylonian myths. Hibil-Ziwa's sojourn in the underworld lasts thousands of years. In the first underworld he finds Ruha. He travels farther in a disguise which no *mana* can penetrate—in this story spirits of darkness are called *manas*. By each king he is given a passport into the territory of the next: one of the talismans is the *skandola*.[3]

[1] Qin, possibly from the root קין, 'to fabricate, work in iron', &c. (hence the Cain of the Bible). A modern translation of Qin might be 'machinist'!

[2] See *GR*, trs. pp. 150 ff. [3] The magic iron ring, see *MMII*, p. 37.

In the world of Anatan and Qin he blinds the guardians of the Well of Darkness 'out of which we proceeded, in which we were formed and came into being',[1] so that they perceive nothing when he communes with the *gimra* (gem, pearl, soul) which lies there crying to him and yearning after him. He takes her and the *mrara* with him, and, appearing as a beautiful stranger to Qin and Anatan, tells them that he comes as suitor for their daughter Zahriel.[2] (Ruha, their other daughter, is wedded to her brother Gaf.[3])

The story of the wedding is related racily and in great detail: it might almost be a description of a betrothal and marriage in the marshes today. Qin is entranced by the suitor's comeliness: he is embraced by Anatan and accepted as future son-in-law. Zahriel describes to her mother the unearthly beauty of the ring he has given her. Guests are bidden to the marriage, a feast made ready, and a wedding-tent and golden bed prepared for the young pair on the nuptial night. At the wedding-feast Hibil-Ziwa merely pretends to eat and drink, and the next morning when, as today, according to custom, the mother visits her daughter to inquire what took place, she hears that the bridegroom did not remove the bride's veil, that is to say, he left her virginity intact. Qin asks anxiously if the bridegroom possesses that which makes a man. Zahriel replies that he does. Questioned by his mother-in-law, Hibil-Ziwa replies that in his country a man waits seven years before a marriage is consummated. By magic, worked by the 'great Mystery' which accompanied him, the seven years are converted into seven thousand myriad years. Qin tells her strange son-in-law secrets of the World of Darkness and how it came into being: 'She saith to me, "We came into being from the Tanna[4] and procreation[5] of the Darkness and from the whole *saka* [extreme, limit] of the Black Waters." '

[1] i.e. the Womb of Matter.
[2] زهرة = 'whiteness, beauty'.
[3] גוף = 'body, person, self'.
[4] Here 'womb'?
[5] *Niṣubta* is a word of wide meaning, 'plant', 'planting', 'implanting', 'propagation', 'fertilization', 'procreation', &c., and in *ATŠ* *nṣab niṣubta* means 'took to wife' or 'performed a marriage'.

In foolish trustfulness she shows him the well in which a magic mirror lies in which they 'behold their faces and know what they intend to do'. Again he deceives her and takes the mirror.

The end of this allegorical fairy-story, for such it is, is long and confused. Zahriel passes out of the picture, yet, as appears from other passages in the book, the unconsummated marriage results in the birth of Pthahil, who thus has within himself a heritage from 'both sides of the family' as child of light and child of darkness. The end of the story is concerned with the woes and perplexities of Zahriel's sister Ruha, who, pregnant of 'Ur by her brother, passes weeping upward through other worlds of darkness. She asks Hibil-Ziwa several times, 'When shall I reach my parents?' But the parents for whom she longs are still not the Parents whom she must one day seek and it is in the worlds of darkness that 'Ur, the Serpent-child, the giant, is born.

I need not follow the myth further: I have told it only to show how the story of Hibil-Ziwa's journey is told in the *GR* and the *šarḥ* scrolls. In the secret literature it is almost ignored. In the *GR*r little is said about the elaborate purifications necessary before Hibil-Ziwa is freed from pollution. The *Niṭufta* ('Drop') immerses him in seven Jordans *after* he has embraced his Father (*GR*r 152: 9), and from that immersion he goes to the Jordan 'of the *Mana* and its Counterpart' (*mana udmuṯh*)

> My father [*here Manda-ḏ-Hiia is meant*] baptized me and pronounced secret signs (*rušumia*) over me. He baptized me in three hundred and sixty thousand myriads of mighty Jordans of white water, and all the 'uthras who were with me. (*GR*r 153: 4 f.)

There is no mention of the 'Letter', or of the Blessed Oblation; only of baptisms, or immersions.

An 'uthra prominent in priestly scrolls is, of course, the 'uthra who is the archetype at once of priest and bridegroom, Šišlam-Rba. The name, like Adakas, is probably a contraction of two words, but what are they?[1] He is the protector of Naṣirutha and

[1] שְׁישׁ (שׁוּשׁ) and עלם? Or a Shafel of šlm?

promotes the welfare of Naṣoraeans both in this world and in the next. He sanctifies the continuance of the race. Both as priest and bridegroom he is crowned, but the bridegroom's crown is a wreath of fig-leaves and myrtle, whilst the priest's crown, a silken fillet, represents the ether-crown which rests on the brow of Adam Kasia (see p. 6). The rituals of ordination and of marriage are described in three priestly scrolls, the Šarḥ ḏ-Taraṣa ḏ-Taga ḏ-Šišlam-Rba, the Šarḥ ḏ-Qabin ḏ-Šišlam-Rba, and a defective section in the *ATŠ* in which the marriage with 'zlat-Rabtia (Great 'zlat) is related in Part V*b*. The marriage of the two is described as a ceremony which reflects the Sacred Union:

And then the Guardian of Mysteries speaketh, saying to the Great Primal Father, the Hidden Radiance: 'O Lofty King to whom 'uthras submit themselves! Reveal this word and tell me what this testimony is like, why it exists and what doth the transplantation[1] resemble? Who amongst 'uthras performed the act of propagation and who will perform it amongst the kings? And when they enact it, which 'uthras should bear testimony about it and who should not witness their word? . . .'

'Then the great Primal Father, the pure Radiance, speaketh and saith to the Guardian of Mystic Rites [Treasures], 'O great Guardian, sublime and ineffable Vine, O good Vine! Turn thine eyes, view the Wellspring and Palmtree from whom Šišlam and 'zlat proceeded. Behold, these [*two*] took one another in marriage just like their Parents, when their Father sought companionship and wished to create 'uthras. (*ATŠ*, trs. pp. 266–7.)

In Part VII of the same manuscript, Šišlam-Rba is called the son of Life 'who standeth at His right hand'. As archetype of priesthood he admonishes and inspires priests, just as a lower type, Yušamin or Yušamin-Rba, typifies the inexpert and careless priest.

And should there be aught of Yušamin—the being whose throne was overturned—in his mind, do thou [O] Šišlam-Rba see to it. For thou art Our sight, thou hast no cause for anxiety, thou dost not fret or trouble thyself as to whether thou wilt be questioned about thy misdoing. Teach thy priest! (*ATŠ*, p. 296.)

[1] *Niṣubta*; see p. 58, n 5.

In the Diwan Malkuta 'laita and in the Coronation prayers all Nature breaks into manifestations of joy when the crown of priesthood is placed on his head: the 'white waters which dwell in the Wellspring' sport and rejoice, the Jordans frolic and dance in *CP* Prayer 307. They say

> Our glory here hath shone out
> It hath shone in this new crown
> The like of which existeth not.
> Blessed is this new crown
> And blessed are its leaves which shall not fall.

The last line indicates that the original 'crown' of priesthood was of living leaves, and not of metal or silk. The priest's insignia are his crown, his gold ring, his staff, and his banner, or perhaps 'regalia' should be the word since he is a king. The banner in the Coronation prayers is called *Šišlamiel*, and in the canonical prayer book twenty canticles are intoned for it. On the other hand, neither Šišlam-Rba nor his banner are mentioned in the *GR*.

The word for 'banner' is Persian not Semitic—*drabša*, pronounced drafsha: it also means 'a ray or beam of light'. In Persian the *dirafsh* (درفش) is a 'banner or standard, a flash of light, or sunrise'. In hymns the banner is always a symbol of light. The Persian origin of the word may offer some clue as to the time when it was adopted as a symbol used in cult or religious ceremony.[1] Professor Henning was good enough to direct my attention to Persian coins. On those of the Frataraka dynasty of Fars, somewhere about 200 B.C., a banner is represented beside a fire-altar: on one set of coins, that of Autophradates the First, the king stands by a large fire-altar in an attitude of worship; the banner is planted on the opposite side of the altar above which is the winged effigy of Ahura Mazda. This banner is square and marked with a cross and four points—probably a sun-symbol.

[1] As a symbol of victory the banner has of course a long past chronicled in Christian art; Jesus holds a banner when issuing from the tomb and the Paschal lamb is depicted with a pennant, symbol of the victory of life over death (the 'Lamb and Flag').

Now such a grouping is familiar to anyone who has watched a Mandaean baptism today, the 'king' of course being the priest. The fire-altar[1] has shrunk to the small but nevertheless essential fire-saucer. The banner is planted beside it just as on the Persian coin, although the pennant part is lengthened considerably.

I think that we have a clue here. The adoption of the banner, together with a great many names of cult objects, vestments, and so on point to Persis or Parthia. Supposing migration to be accepted as possible, was all this adopted before or after migration? Possibly the latter? Ṭīb[2] was the centre of the cult at the time of the Moslem invasion, and Yāqūt, in *Mu'ajjam al-Buldān*, mentions the report that Ṭīb 'was one of the residences of Seth, son of Adam, and that the inhabitants of the town never ceased to confess the religion of Seth' (i.e. Mandaean Šitil). He also says that they were Nabataeans speaking Nabataean (i.e. Aramaic).

Fars is actually mentioned in the second of the banner hymns, (*CP*, No. 330):

> In the name of the Great Life!
> When Radiance emerged from the white land Faris,
> [*i.e. Fars, Persis*]
> A youth, Arsfan, unfurled a banner:
> He unfurled a great radiance
> So that 'uthras and *škintas* shone in its glory.
> They shone in the brightness of his banner
> Like radiance in the House of the Mighty.

Can it be deduced from this hymn, from the silence of the *GR* on the subject of the banner and its omission of Šišlam's name, that both are accretions due to an Iranian environment after emigration to the south-east, and that Šišlam is a late aggrandisement of the sacerdotal caste?

Whether we consider Šišlam a figure of later cult or not,

[1] Little is said in Mandaean texts about the fire although it is always present and necessary for the incense and for baking the sacramental bread. Its purity is strictly preserved (see p. 113) and in *ATŠ* we read that 'a baptism without fire will not ascend to the House of Life'.

[2] The town has now disappeared: it lay in a well-watered district between the marshes of southern Iraq and the Jebel Hamrīn. See p. 105, n. 2.

Yawar, or Yawar-Ziwa, certainly belongs to an older stratum. The hymn cycle 'When the Proven Pure One went', part of which appears in *GR*, represents him as the 'uthra to whom is entrusted the creation of the ether-world and its inhabitants. Most of the canticles of the series are recited at every wedding and at the 'coronation' of a priest. The root from which his name is derived, 'UR or AWR, has a double meaning, 'to blind or dazzle with light' or 'to awaken'. The basic idea, perhaps, is that light falling on the eyes of a sleeper causes him to awake. Hence as a spirit of dazzling light, who wakens to life and to light, he appears in the gnostic cosmology as one of the first emanations. In Hymn 374 we see him in all his glory:

> I worship, praise and laud
> The four hundred and forty-four thousand names
> Of Yawar-Ziwa, son of Nbaṭ-Ziwa,[1]
> King of *'uthras*, great Viceregent
> Of *škinata* (*sanctuaries*, *shekinahs*)
> Chief over mighty and celestial worlds
> Of radiance, light and glory;
> Who is within the Veil, within his own *škinta*,
> Before whom no being existed.

His spouse, Simat-Hiia, 'Treasure of Life', has already been mentioned; the pair are often invoked together.

Names with Ziwa (Radiance) as part of them seem to be aspects or functions of Primal Light. Hibil-Ziwa, for instance, seems to typify the enlightenment of Man, Hibil being one of the sons of Adam, which explains his occasional identification with Manda-ḏ-Hiia (Knowledge-of-Life) (e.g. *ATŠ*, p. 140, No. 114), for one 'uthra is often equated with another when their respective functions overlap. Occasionally Hibil-Ziwa appears as a counterpart of Yawar-Ziwa (Dazzling or Awaking Radiance); they sometimes converse together, as a man will with himself (*ATŠ*, p. 210). This identification of one 'uthra with another often happens with Mara-ḏ-Rabutha (Lord of Greatness), partly

[1] *Nbaṭ*: the root NBṬ means 'to spring forth, burst forth', 'spring upward' &c.

owing to the double meaning of *rabuta*, which means not only 'greatness', 'magnificence', but has a technical meaning. A *rba* is a priest who initiates candidates for the priesthood, and his office is termed *rabuta*. *Rba* then becomes synonymous with 'master', 'teacher', like the Jewish Rabbi, and as a title is written *Rbai* So-and-So. It is extremely difficult to detect, when *Mara-ḏ-Rabuta* is mentioned in a text, whether the allusion is to the priestly teacher or to the divine Teacher, Adam Kasia.

Connexion between one 'uthra and another is often indicated by the word *br*, 'son of', or *ab*, 'father'. They have of course no literal meaning but they show that the beings named are close in personified relationship one to another or, rather, are aspects of each other.

Manda-ḏ-Hiia, literally 'gnosis of Life', is, therefore, quite often identified with Mara-ḏ-Rabutha. His function clearly expressed by his name, he is usually a teacher of the true doctrine, for instance, in *GR*r, book 11, he instructs Anuš (Biblical Enos) thus: (267.) 'Come, I will reveal to thee about the detestable mysteries of this world, which thou hast seen', &c. It is curious that in so long and important a document as *ATŠ* (and other secret scrolls) he is hardly mentioned at all, save in quotations, or when identified with Mara-ḏ-Rabutha. I suspect that he belongs to the same era of composition as Pthahil, who is also considered negligible in the secret scrolls.

Abatur, pronounced Awathur, is a mystery-figure and the meaning of his name uncertain. He is sometimes called the 'Third Life'. Andreas, according to Wilhelm Brandt,[1] derived the name from old Persian words meaning 'provided with (or "possessing") weighing-scales'.[2] If so, the second part of his name *ḏ-muzania*, which distinguishes him from the higher counterpart, is repetitive, for it too means 'of the scales'. His ideal counterpart is *Abatur Rama*, the 'Lofty Abathur'. The parallel with the Egyptian weigher of souls is obvious; the Persian Meher Davar at the Činvat (Bridge of the Requiter) also weighs

[1] W. Brandt, *Die jüdischen Baptismen* (Töpelmann, Giessen, 1910), p. 147.
[2] See *JB*, p. xxix.

the deeds of souls before they may pass over it into worlds of bliss.

Purely allegorical are (*a*) *Kušṭa*, a personification of truth, sincerity, and vows and also of the ritual handshake which symbolizes good faith, and (*b*) *Habšaba*, 'first of the week', Sunday. Minor allegorical figures abound, for instance *Nbaṭ* or *Nbaṭ-Hiia* or *Nṣab-Hiia* ('Life-burst-forth', 'They-planted-Life', &c.). *Abad-ukšar* (He-acted-and-succeeded) is one such name: all or most of which refer to activities and emanations of Life.

One most important 'uthra, Bihram, however, must be considered separately because he is so closely associated with the rite of baptism. His name is Iranian (Avestan Vəδəθraγna) and the Mandaean Bihram may be the Persian genius of victory (New Persian *Bahrām* < Middle Persian *Varhrān*). He has a Yašt to himself and the original form of his name, Verethragna, is, according to Professor E. Benveniste, best rendered as 'celui qui abat la résistance', i.e. 'victor'.[1] Water entered into Verethragna's cult. The presence of the banner at Mandaean baptism may be connected with Bihram's banner of victory, to which I have referred on p. 61 f.

The words pronounced by St. John the Baptist over his candidates for baptism are not chronicled in the gospels. Those pronounced by the Mandaean baptist are these:

Thou art signed with the name of Life: the name of Life and the name of Knowledge-of-life [Manda-ḏ-Hiia] are pronounced over thee. Thou art baptized with the baptism of the great Bihram son of the Mighty. Thy baptism shall protect thee and shall succeed [*be efficacious*]. The name of the Life and the name of Knowledge-of-Life are pronounced upon thee.

[1] For a more recent view see I. Gershevitch, *The Avestan Hymn to Mithra* (Cambridge, 1959), pp. 153–62.

VIII

MYSTERIES AND THE GREAT MYSTERY

SCROLLS intended for the instruction of priests deal chiefly with such subjects as qualification, status, authority, and ordination (coronation); priests consult them in order to discover what must be done to atone for errors in recitation or ritual or to find out what will restore to office a priest who has incurred pollution or committed an involuntary crime against ritual law. They deal also with the correct performance of all rites and religious ceremonies. In these scrolls, therefore, there is only an occasional hint or reference to the inner meaning attached to ritual acts. Nevertheless, when these are set together a picture gradually emerges. Each *raza*, each 'mystery', is a drama, and the actions performed by its celebrant express in mime and symbol what that 'mystery' represents and what effect each sacrament has on the soul for whose benefit it is performed. Scrolls intended for perusal in the hut of initiation are more outspoken, but they are still couched in the language of parable and symbol, so obscure in expression that none but a 'true Naṣoraean' can interpret its meaning. The mysteries of Naṣirutha are reserved for men who realize that the *arcana* must be hidden from the unworthy although these embody truths essential to the understanding of religion.

Baptism is the foundation of the whole redemptive system: it is spiritual rebirth. It cleanses body and soul and symbolizes rising into a new life: the ascent to the bank after immersion is symbolic. It is an individual act—though there may be several candidates, only one at a time descends into the water, just as later on a man or woman goes down into death alone. They are still in the physical body (the *'ṣṭun pagria*). When on the bank they wait with others who have been baptized for the sacramental bread and water[1] and the signing with sesame oil, this conveys the lesson that whilst they are still 'in the body' they share with fellow believers the higher life into which baptism admits them. Hence the unction and communal meal of baptism represent a *laufa*, a union or communion. The bread itself is a 'mystery'. The wheat is brought, selected, washed, dried, and ground in a quern by the priest in the *mandi* or other purified place. He has previously immersed himself, robed, and said the preliminary prayers. He mixes the flour with salt (called 'the mystery of the soul'), wets it with 'Jordan' (running) water, and bakes it just before the baptism on a fire-saucer used for this purpose and for burning incense. Of the breaking of bread as a symbol of creation we have already spoken (p. 3). The banner planted by the fire is a symbol of light and of Bihram[2] and the gold twisted beneath its peak is a sun-metal symbolical of the Father.

In this world baptism is a protection: it wards off evil spirits, disease-demons, and the attack of inauspicious planets. In the next it is all-important, for the soul 'which descended into the water and was baptized' has been 'signed with the Pure Sign', 'signed with the Sign of Life'. When the departed soul arrives at the frontier guarded by Abathur,[3] she displays it as a passport prompted by the guardian with whom she has been provided.

All those souls who were signed with the Sign of Life will be met by a guardian. If not, the soul's deeds will accompany her and bear her company until, at the frontier-house, her evil deeds stand revealed. (*ATŠ*, p. 264.)

[1] The Jewish Christians, the Ebionites, used water not wine in the baptism sacrament, which use some early Church writers confused with the sacraments of the mass, as did, apparently, Irenaeus (*Ag. Her.*, bk. V, i, A-N Library, vol. ii, p. 57): 'Therefore do these men reject the commixture of the heavenly wine and wish it to be water of the world only . . .', &c.

[2] See p. 61. 'Verehan (Bihram) created by Ahura-Mazda who bears the standard of glory created by Ahura-Mazda' (V, xix. 125).

[3] 'And on she went and reached Abathur's house of detention, the Ancient, Lofty, Holy, and Guarded One. There his scales are set up and spirits and souls are questioned before him as to their names, their Signs, their blessing, their baptism and everything that goes therewith' (*CP* 49).

Only once is the rite of baptism[1] an admission rite and that is the first baptism of an infant; for baptism must be constantly repeated as a cleansing from pollution,[2] is performed before and after marriage, at every major festival, and is essential before death.

O my good child, to these questions that thou hast asked (*know*) that the Jordan cleanses: it is the father of all worlds, celestial, medial, and lower. It is a medicine transcending all means of healing. (Ibid., p. 150.)

Sunday is the day on which baptisms are usually performed, and during the five intercalary days baptism is performed daily, as these days are 'days of light'.[3]

The Mandaean sacraments form a graduated series of symbolical acts, each of which must be performed in a state of purity, and each of which reminds the individual that he is a member of the *kana ḏ-nišmata*, which could be rendered 'the Family (*lit. stem* or *group*) of Souls'. Such is the simple ritual meal called *Laufa*, 'union' or 'communion'—*lofani*[4] in the vernacular. This is a communal ritual eating of bread and drinking of water followed by other foods symbolic of life. It is celebrated after death at the graveside or at intervals after death by mourners, and the immaterial double of the food consumed by them is supposed to be eaten by the spirit of the deceased whose death is commemorated as well as by those of any other dead persons whose names are mentioned with his, with the

[1] Baptism does not replace self-immersion, which should take place after any pollution such as child-birth, sexual connexion, menstruation, &c., and is also curative of certain forms of illness, such as lunacy. Cf. Peter (in *H*, IX, chap. xix), who says that evil spirits and disease (-*demons*) can be driven out by 'washing in a flowing river or fountain or even in the sea'.

[2] Serious pollution, for a priest, entails 360 baptisms 'from Sunday to Sunday', and until thus purified he may take part in no rite, not even as assistant.

[3] Baptism is described in *MMII*, chap. vii: its institution, p. 127, after child-birth, pp. 43–44; of a child, pp. 44–46 and 81–92; of a dead child, p. 46; after marriage, pp. 65, 71, &c. Mandaean baptism as a whole is discussed in Dr. E. Segelberg's *Maṣbuta* (Uppsala, 1958), and for the general background see R. Reitzenstein's *Die Vorgeschichte der christlichen Taufe* (Berlin) and W. Brandt's *Die jüdischen Baptismen*. For a Mandaean source, see *MḏHZ*.

[4] For *laufa* (*lofani*) see *MMII*, pp. 59–72.

formula '*Laufa uruaha d̲-hiia ušabiq haṭaiih nihuilh̲* ('Union, refreshment of life and forgiving of sins be there for him'—*or her*).

Next in importance to this quasi-lay sacramental meal comes the *zidqa brika*, the 'Blessed Oblation'. The name covers several different forms of the sacrament. In all of them, together with unleavened loaves (round), fruit, and other ritual foods, bread appears in an unusual shape. It is the *ṣa*, emblematic of the Father. This may be either (*a*) two flaps of bread rolled together[1] in a tight scroll into which the celebrant inserts morsels of ritual food all symbolic of fertility, or it may be (*b*) a solid, sausage-shaped lump of unleavened dough about four or five inches long. Both appear to be models of the phallus.[2] The first type, (*a*), of *ṣa* is used at the wedding sacrament: when broken in two, half is eaten by the bridegroom and half by the bride. A second Oblation is celebrated after the wedded pair have been purified by baptism. An account of the wedding Oblation is given in detail in *MMII*, pp. 59–72, and need not be repeated here. Priestly commentaries on and descriptions of a heavenly wedding are given in a section of *ATŠ* and in the *Šd̲Q*.

I have found in none of the ritual scrolls in my possession a definite indication of what, at these Oblations, symbolizes the 'Mother'. Commentators state that at the *masiqta* her womb is represented by the cup or bowl of freshly drawn water into which grapes or raisins have been macerated; hence it is likely that the wine-cup similarly prepared at the Oblations is also representative of her reproductive power. Dates (*sindirka*) added to the wedding cup only intensify that power, for to the 'Mother'

[1] *Trin faṭiria mlabšin bhdadia* (Diwan Maṣbuta Rabtia, line 132).

[2] In the Diwan Maṣbuta Rabtia, line 139 f., the *ṣa* is called 'this great First *Sindirka*', i.e. the male date-palm, which (see pp. 7 ff.) is the symbol of the phallus. A similar object of phallic shape appears in a Nestorian rite (see *WW*, pp. 70 ff.) which apparently represents the conception of the Virgin Mary. The word *ṣa* is probably the Aramaic צָעָא, 'a dish', for it cannot be the alternative 'filth'. The similarity of the first type of *ṣa* to the Jewish *Kuraikh* (as it is called in 'Iraq), the round thin loaf rolled into a scroll with lettuce which is dipped into vinegar or lemon juice and eaten at the *seder* meal at Passover, must occur to anyone who has witnessed both rites, the Mandaean and the Jewish.

the life-bestowing power of the 'Father' (Date-palm) has been added to the 'wine'. The *Zidqa brika* after death and that celebrated after the *masiqta* on the fifth intercalary day have been described by me in *MMII*, pp. 190 and 205 ff., as well as the Oblation at the *Ahaba ḏ-mania* (ibid., pp. 214–22). Commentaries enumerate what should be placed on the various Oblation tables: for a wedding (Bodleian Library MS. *DC* 38), salt, *ṭabuta* (bread), green edible stuff, fish, *sindirka* (dates), grapes, nuts, sesame mixed with salt, and *hamra* (the mixed cup described above); the *ṣa* (type (*b*)) is made during the ceremony. At the Oblation for the Great Baptism (to reinstate a disqualified priest)—salt, *ṭabuta* (bread), green salad or vegetables, fish, *sindirka* (dates), pomegranate, quince, myrtle, *hamra* in a bottle, and a bowl. The *hamra* is prepared just before the ceremony. The *ṣa* is made in the manner first described and the celebrant is told to place in it as much of the fruit as he can. Both these Oblations are for living persons. The *ṣa* for the Oblation after burial is solid and no nuts or fruit are inserted, nor are they in the *Ahaba ḏ-mania*, for both are celebrated for the dead, not for the living.

The words, as given in the Bodleian manuscript *DC* 50, said by the celebrant, when holding the *ṣa* and breaking it into two (or more pieces if there are concelebrants), are:

> 'In the name of the Great Life! Union [*laufa*] and renewal [*ruaha*] of life and forgiving of sins be there for this soul of N.' And break [*it*] and say 'by [*means of*] this treasure [*ginza*], these prayers and this baptism and Blessed Oblation, and by this, the Great First Date-palm[1] consumed in communion [*mitlif*]; and by [*means of*] these wholesome fruits of this *masiqta*.' (Diwan Maṣbuta Rabtia, lines 135 ff.)

This is, quite clearly, an invocation of the 'Father'.

To illustrate how the scrolls describe the celebration of an Oblation in narrative form I will quote from *ARR*. The soul of Adam Kasia is being 'raised' by the ceremony.

> So he hearkened to the Word and took white sesame from the bank

[1] See p. 69, n. 2 and p. 71, n. 4.

of the spring and brought wheat, walnuts, grapes, pomegranate, and quince, and brought [*also*] a 'good brother' [*dove*] for the soul.[1]

Then He [*the Word*] came with Adam and thereupon they began and built a sanctuary [*bimanda*] of pure crystal, because BIMANDA is composed [*spelt*] of seven letters. Then they soused the *bimanda*.

And they took the wheat, a quern and fuel from mulberry trees and took in the white sesame, pounded it and extracted its oil. And they kneaded and pressed bread with oil like the anointing of the wreath.

Then they folded and wrapped the *pandama*[2] over their mouths. Thus did they make preparations until the dawn.

The Ayar-Dakia [Pure-Ether] arose and descended into the spring and lifted out a small fish from the spring and they boiled [*it*?] and set up a Table of pure crystal. Next they brought a dish [*patura*][3] and the mystery of *sindirka*,[4] green vegetables and the leaves of beans and some of the herbs which sprout at the brink of the spring. Then they stood and consecrated their crowns when the seven vestments[5] had been put on.

Then they brought the symbol [*raza*] of the soul. that is to say salt, which [*word*] is composed of five letters, namely MIHLA which is a symbol of the soul's girdle, for anything not girt in by a boundary [*lit.* bounded by a girdle] is unstable, infirm, perisheth and is held back [*i.e. in darkness*].

Then they held the dish, two unleavened loaves, one for the Mother and one for the Father,[6] and then said 'Union and revival [*ruaha*] of life and forgiving of sins be there for this soul—' and paused, not knowing what they should say.[7]

However, the Lofty King knew what was in their minds, so he sent Bihdad the Messenger and a letter was carried in his hand. He came towards them and put the letter into the hand of Pure-Ether who

[1] The dove was not brought for the Oblation, but in readiness for the *masiqta* which is described as following the Oblation.

[2] The lower part of the face is veiled.

[3] *Patura* = 'table', 'dish', or any flat, clean surface upon which food is laid.

[4] Here this is the *ṣa*, referred to later as the *pihla* (phallus), see p. 72, n. 2.

[5] i.e. the rasta, see *MMII*, pp. 30–39.

[6] Preparations for the *masiqta* known as *Dabahata* (of the Parents) according to this MS. preceded the Oblation; hence the two loaves and the dove (not used at the preliminary rite).

[7] As Primal Man was as yet nameless, and the soul for whom a rite is celebrated must be mentioned by name together with the name of his mother (N. son of N.), a name and fictitious mother's name was inserted by the celestial celebrants.

thereupon kissed it 360 times, opened it, read it, and gazed at its sublime words.

And so they bestowed on him [*Adam Kasia*] the name 'Adam-Shaq-Ziwa son of Himat-Razia' [*and continued*] 'of this raising-up', and said 'Union and revival of life and forgiving of sins be there for this soul of Adam-Shaq-Ziwa son of Himat-Razia.'

And they broke [*bread*] and ate three morsels with salt: they ate these and drank [*water*]. And then they brought three unleavened loaves and placed them on the Table and said 'In the name of the Life and in the name of Knowledge-of-Life may the *ṭabuta* [bounty][1] of Life and the *ṭabuta* of Knowledge-of-Life be accepted, and the *pihla ḏ-'l šum hiia pla.*[2] (*ARR*, lines 166–87.)

This narrative continues without a break to a description of the first *masiqta* performed by the divine celebrants for the soul of Archetypal Man.

In this book I am not concerned with the manner in which the sacraments are performed but with their interpretation according to Naṣirutha. The actual performance of the *masiqta* is described in full detail in *WW*. It is, of course, easy to recognize in many details of these rites ancient fertility magic, which, in the marriage sacrament lies behind the insertion of seeds and scraps of prolific fruits in the bread eaten by the pair—they hope to have children. The true Naṣoraean, unperturbed by such an identification, would readily assent and accept, for he knows and understands the language of symbol and would find in this nothing to offend his worship of the Great Life. Asceticism is abhorrent to him, to carry on the gift of life is the will of the Great Life. Although to the soul the body is a prison, she accepts and is grateful for the good gifts which sweeten her exile. They are meant to be used and enjoyed, not to be misused or rejected. Man may take pleasure in those things which delight his soul; beauty, the warmth of sun in winter, pure air, the green shade of trees, the fragrance of flowers, sexual intercourse within

[1] In the ritual manuscripts *ṭabuta* (goodness, benefaction, bounty, &c.) often means 'bread' and is so understood. Sometimes, however, it refers to all the food on the ritual table.

[2] i.e. 'the phallus which . . . (?) at the name of the Life'. The reference appears to be to the *ṣa*, but translation of this phrase is still doubtful.

marriage,[1] which should be early, the begetting of children and delight in them; the finer pleasures of the senses,[2] but not lust; eating and drinking, but neither greed nor fasting. The *GR* is full of precepts urging moderation and condemning celibacy and mortification of the flesh. When a man prays for forgiveness of sins, in the next breath he prays for 'joy of heart'.

The approach of death should be welcomed if an absolutely pure life has been led, but too often it is accompanied by dread, for, no matter how innocent a life a man has led, he faces peril. His death must be ritually 'clean', he must neither be naked nor wear ordinary clothes—at the moment of passing he must face the north, and, above all, a priest and his assistant must be present for the last rites. Otherwise his soul may be held back or pass into torment.

The sacrament for the dying, called 'the Letter', is undoubtedly ancient. As I said earlier, it is referred to in the Syriac 'Song of the Soul'. It is fully described in the book of liturgical prayers and hymns and I was given an account of it which can be read in *MMII*; but when writing that book I did not realize that the ceremony should be performed for every dying person. A candidate for the ganzivrate must have been present at such a ceremony for a 'perfect' (see p. 43, n. 2) before he is finally consecrated in office. Nowadays it is rarely performed *in toto* because priests are few and often far, so that to summon a priest and an *ašganda* (acolyte) to a deathbed in time is usually impracticable. Part of the rite is performed in most cases. As soon as the relatives of a gravely ill person think that death is imminent, and often while life hangs in the balance, he or she is dressed in

[1] According to Epiphanius, early marriage was enjoined by Judaeo-Christians (Nazarenes) and by the Elkasaites. With Mandaeans polygamy is allowed, although infrequent. Women can take only one husband and re-marriage is against religion. A widow, divorcee, and a girl not a virgin cannot be married by a priest—only by a *paisaq* (see *MMII*, p. 173). Women are a constant danger to ritual purity whenever Nature brings them into states of uncleanness: moreover, they belong to the Left, and Ruha, therefore, has more power over women than over men.

[2] Music, dancing, and the wearing of colours and jewels are frowned upon in *GR*. This is probably because professional musicians and dancers were thought to have light morals.

the *rasta* (religious white dress) and immersed thrice. The immersion may be either in the river or baptismal pool, or water may be drawn from either running source and there and then poured three times over his or her body. The death is then 'clean' and what is lacking may be atoned for later, usually during the five intercalary days, by *dukrana* ('mentioning') at ritual meals and Blessed Oblations. Should death overtake a Mandaean whilst not dressed in the *rasta* or naked, an *Ahaba ḏ-mania* rite must be performed and a *masiqta* is desirable.

In the chapter on Adam Kasia much has already been said about the *masiqta*, the mystery of mysteries. We have seen that it symbolizes the creation of the Secret Adam, the cosmic Adam, limb by limb in the primeval vastness of the cosmic Womb, the Mother.[1] Just as his embryo was developed and built up until the whole Archetypal Man was formed, so, by invocation of those tremendous cosmic powers, is the soul of the deceased provided bit by bit with a spiritual body. With Man and in the Divine Man, he is born again. Were St. Paul's words (1 Cor. xv. 22) to be slightly altered, they could be those of a Naṣoraean —'For as in Adam all die, even so in the *Secret Adam* shall all be made alive.'

The *masiqta* is so holy that lay eyes may not witness it, so sacredly dangerous that the least slip, the least omission, must be expiated by baptisms and repeated *masiqtas*.[2] The gravest mistakes such as those which concern the 'semination' (pouring water into the wine-cup) may disqualify a priest for life. In *WW* I recorded as faithfully as I could how modern priests celebrate the rite. But they did not tell me the symbolic meaning of the actions they performed and for reasons explained in the Epilogue I have sometimes wondered if they really knew. The *ATŠ* and the *ARR* and the other secret texts describe the first archetypal *masiqta* celebrated for Adam Kasia. The *ARR* begins

[1] Commentaries on the *masiqta* use the words 'Father' and 'Mother' of the two cosmic powers during the 'sacred marriage'.

[2] *ATŠ* in *Mhita uasuta* specifies errors and omissions committed during celebration, and enumerates the baptisms and *masiqtas* necessary to atone for such faults.

with a 'Blessed Oblation' (see pp. 70 ff.) and continues without a break to describe the celebration of the greater mystery.

Today, a *masiqta* should be celebrated by a *ganzibra* (head priest, chief celebrant), two priests, and an *ašganda*.[1] The *masiqta* described in *ARR* appears to have only two celebrants, Ayar-Rba (Great Ether) sometimes called Ayar Dakia (Pure-Ether) as *ganzibra*, Mahzian-the-Word as concelebrant, and a spirit called Bihdad as *ašganda*. The Body of Archetypal Man is, apparently, still theoretically unformed; I cannot explain this confusing assumption. Throughout the *masiqta* he is called Adam-Shaq-Ziwa[2] son of Himat-Razia,[3] for in an earthly *masiqta* the name of the mother must be given. His soul, that of future humanity, since man is not yet created, is pictured as bodiless, anxiously watching the mysteries and impatiently awaiting the 'ninth month' when the divinely-conceived Body is given birth. The rites up to the time of birth are described as being 'of the Mother'.

The second part of the *masiqta*, which is supposed to mime the baptism of the soul, her anointing with the chrism and the provision of viaticum for her journey towards the worlds of light, is, according to the running commentary, 'of the Father'.

The narrative shall be quoted from the point when the *qnasa* performed outside the sanctuary (see p. 31) is accomplished: the slaughter of the dove in silence has taken place:

They cleansed it [the dove's body], brought the mystery of salt and put with it, cooked it and took it over to the *bimanda*.[4] Then they entered the *bimanda* and each [*celebrant*] put on his vestments; set his table before him and placed thereon the *faṭiria*,[5] the dove's flesh and

[1] See pp. 73, 107.

[2] 'Adam-was-bright-Radiance' (שחק, 'to be bright, to laugh', is paralleled by צחק, 'to laugh or smile'). 'Now it is a most typical feature of El in Ugaritic literature that he "laughs", *yṣḥq* . . .' G. Widengren, 'Early Hebrew Myths', in *Myth, Ritual and Kingship*, ed. S. H. Hooke (Clarendon Press, Oxford, 1958), p. 187.

[3] 'On-account-of-Mysteries'?

[4] See p. 2, n. 4.

[5] Small disks of unsalted unleavened bread made and passed through fire before the priests enter the sanctuary.

the myrtle and put the *miša*[1] in a crystal cup. And each [*celebrant*] brought incense and set it before him and placed grapes in his bowl. And he carried his crown and his staff in his left and two phials in his right hand. And he filled them [*at the Jordan?*] and put the phial of *halalta* [*rinsing water*] on the bank of the spring and placed the other before him on the table and put a walnut on the mouth of the phial.

It is unnecessary to continue, for the rite proceeds, with only slight difference, as described in *WW*, pp. 242–58. It is to the commentaries that we now look for explanation of the rite. As the *masiqta* performed by Adam is the first of its kind, and as yet there are, supposedly, no human beings, the sixty *faṭiria* on the ritual table (which today represent the souls of the dead) are explained as 'souls of sixty priests' due to come into earthly existence in the far distant future: 'thirty from the world of the Father and thirty from the world of the Mother'. Liturgical prayers are quoted as milestones or landmarks; the commentary running thus:

And when thou takest the phial and recitest over it 'Ye are waters of Life',[2] thou rousest the Semen which seeketh to fall down into the Womb, for thou prayest a command to shed water on the earth.' (*ARR numeration of lines impossible because of illustrations*).

ATŠ comments at this stage:[3]

The First Semen is thus glorified and a force created more sublime than any of the forces which develop from it, for it is marrow, it is that which was formed before all other mysteries. And then seven (*sic*) others follow, the bone, flesh, sinews, veins, skin and hair. (*ATS*, nos. 113–14.)

(The *masiqta* described[4] is one with seven celebrants and a mysterious eighth.)

. . . These seven (are?) *faṭiria* upon which they, the seven priests, recited. And those two others are the spirit and the soul: the eighth

[1] Oil of unction, see p. 31. A small bowl of this must be on each altar-table for unction of the loaves after morsels of sacred food have been placed on them. (Only one of these loaves represents, after special treatment, the soul for whom the *masiqta* is celebrated.)

[2] *CP* 33, *ML* xxxiii, p. 62. In all commentaries the liturgical prayers are quoted in their present form.

[3] i.e. the stage at which the priest pours water into the wine-cup.

[4] It is a *masiqta* called the *Masiqta of Šitil* (Seth).

loaf is that of the spirit and the seventh that of the soul. (*ATŠ*, pt. iv, no. 114.)

(*One would expect the soul to be ninth!*)

The explanations given by the priestly commentators are involved: it often seems as if they were reading from a palimpsest, in which first one writing and then another were visible. The reason is, that the *faṭiria*, as representative of the Body of Adam, symbolize, not only the souls of the dead awaiting their light-bodies, but also that Body, of which they as human beings form part, the limbs and organs, the spirits of light which govern them— the spiritual powers of the cosmos.

ARR uses Persian words when describing the 'semination':

And when the Semen falleth on the blood in the Womb,[1] it purifieth the blood and maketh it of one nature with Itself so that there is no darkness therein. And when thou makest the three passes[2] thou placest three names upon it [*i.e. the faṭira*] 'which are MUHR, RŠT and RST'.[3] And these are various epithets of Yawar-Ziwa.

ARR enumerates organs and limbs at great length, for, should any mistake occur, the 'light-body' would be injured.

After the water has been poured into the wine-cup, the commentaries liken what follows to the nine months of gestation. The Great-Ether says to Adam Kasia:

Note that there are nine Ṭab ṭabias,[4] one for each month till the infant is developed, stage by stage until, at the ninth month, Pure-Ether comes and enters into it and turns its head downwards. Because every soul that leaveth the body descends downward—and then rejoices, seeks grace, leaps up and rises towards Me.

Behold, O My Plant, Thou, my Good Plant, Thou didst go below,

[1] The belief that conception takes place when male semen unites with blood in the womb appears in the Clementine Homilies, e.g. III. xxvii, 'for the female surrounding the white seed of the male with her own blood, as with red fire, sustains her own weakness with the extraneous support of bones'.

[2] See *WW*, pp. 251 f. The triple pass, from left to right, is made five times over each *faṭira*.

[3] In *GR* 26 Abathur is identified with Rašna and Rast: see *GR*, trs., p. 284, nn. 2 and 4. According to Lidzbarski (*GR*, trs., p. 284, n. 4, followed by Zaehner, *Zurvan*, p. 77) these names represent the Iranian triad Mithra, Sraoša, and Rašnu).

[4] The commemoration prayer for the dead, *CP* 72, and the longer version *CP* 170.

didst assume kingliness and camest towards Me. And then thou didst create worlds at Thy right hand and at Thy left hand.[1]

And Ether (*Ayar*) arrangeth all before Thee, and Father Jordan giveth drink behind Thee. (*ARR.*)

Then birth takes place and the babe breathes.

And that incense which thou castest in the first section is that pure ether which entered and brought that babe from the small womb into the great womb. And it looketh yearningly towards its baptism so that it can breathe the Breath of Life and [be signed] with the Sign of the Jordan.

Up to this [*point*] the first part is set out, that is the Mother.[2] She is the Earth which bringeth forth fruits and seeds and looketh to the cloud, that is the sky, which bringeth rain and dew, to impart to her some of its mysteries. Should cloud not bestow rain upon her, the earth becomes hot upon her [*seeds*] and devours them.

Behold, Earth is the Mother and the worlds of light the Father. And that [*first*] section, [*that*] of the sixty *faṭiria* concerns the Mother. But the section of '*ḏ-abahatan*'[3] concerns the Father: it is that in which there are many signings and passes. (*ARR.*)

Now the soul is freed from earth, her prison, and is reborn into a spiritual body. The purified *ruha* unites with her 'sister' the soul. Baptized, signed, and provided with viaticum, both soar heavenward 'as one'.

And when thou recitest 'Praises to the Outer Life'[4] she openeth her eyes and gazeth at the heavens in which she placeth her trust. And when thou recitest 'Thou, Life'[5] she setteth off and flieth into the firmament. And when thou recitest 'Communion and renewal of Life'[6] and 'Lifting eyes'[7] she is clad in the mysteries of the Father so that none of the purgatory demons [*maṭaraiia*][7] can block her way. (*ARR.*)

[1] Here we get the 'descent' of Adam, i.e. when his physical and lower counterpart appears in the world of matter. The ascent is the rise of humanity as a whole into the spiritual. Here, very plainly, we perceive the Messiah-Saviour theme.

[2] In the Orthodox Mass the rite at the prothesis altar ends with the birth of the Holy Child. It could, like the first part of the *masiqta*, be described as 'of the Mother'. The next stage of the mass takes place at the high altar, and, again like the *masiqta*, ends with 'resurrection'. See *WW*, pp. 123–34, and for the water into wine, pp. 75–77.

[3] The longer of the two commemoration prayers, *CP* 170 (not in *ML*).

[4] *CP* 76, *ML* lxxvi, p. 133.

[5] *CP* 77, *ML* lxxvii, p. 141.

[6] *CP* 9, *ML* ix, p. 15, and a phrase constantly used of the dead.

[7] See *CP*, p. 31.

The soul 'on wings of ether' is on her way to Abathur's scales, confident that the *masiqta* has cleansed and redeemed her, for she is wearing the glorious robe of Yuzaṭaq-Manda-ḏ-Hiia.[1]

Throughout any *masiqta* the priest assumes the identity of the soul for whom the *masiqta* is celebrated. The expression in Mandaic is curious, he is 'clothed in', that is acts as, the soul of the departed. Before the *masiqta* actually begins, priests baptize each other and partake of the simple baptism sacrament of bread (salted) and water. This is repeated, minus the baptism, in the cult-hut as soon as the *masiqta* is over.

The *pihta* (sacramental bread) he consumes in character of the departed is one of the *faṭiria* into which, like the others, small pieces of the ritual food and a sliver of dove's flesh has been added. It is brought into connexion with the other loaves by adding to it fragments from two of the piles of *faṭiria* which lie before him. Before it is swallowed by the celebrant, the *pihta* is wrapped about a myrtle wreath, unwrapped, signed with *miša* (oil) dipped into the wine-cup, and consumed whole. Then the priest drinks the 'wine' and the water which rinses the cup.

Throughout this very elaborate and lengthy ritual the priest is terrified of making a mistake. Should he do so, not only would he injure the soul he represents, whose spiritual body may be maimed, but he himself will suffer. Penalties are heavy, graver omissions or mistakes may be punished by degradation to lay status. He is as responsible as a chemist making a dangerous compound. Not only may he spoil what he is making, but he may blow himself up!

If he goeth wrong, and signeth at one of them or both of them [*i.e. two prayers to be recited*] blindness in the eyes and deafness in the ears resulteth. (*ATŠ*, p. 208.)

The deadliest sin of all is an error at the moment when water from the phial on his table (the 'inner phial') is to be poured into the wine-bowl. A priest who uses the wrong phial, or spills the

[1] *Yuzaṭaq* (meaning [*Male*] Holy Spirit?) is an epithet of Manda-ḏ-Hiia (Knowledge of Life).

water, or pours it in at the wrong moment, renders the whole *masiqta* void.

Should this occur, the priests are inhibited. They shall recite and complete that *masiqta*, [*but*] that soul hath become, as it were, an outcast (*ganiba*) and that fluid [*in the wine-cup*] like a woman who received seed from a man not her husband, committed adultery, became pregnant, and the child she bore him became outcast. That priest must be baptized in new vestments by five priests and shall pray sixty *Rahmia* so that the flaw in him shall not persist. And for that soul he must celebrate sixty *masiqtas*. (*ATŠ*, p. 207, No. 35.)

The commentaries vary, but follow the main line of explanation. Over-elaboration is characteristic and it is often difficult to follow or disentangle one metaphor from another. The *ARR* is one of the simpler commentaries: that is the reason why I chose it.

This most solemn of all rites remains a profound experience to the devout, a supreme act of faith and worship.

And Mara-ḏ-Rabutha[1] set Himself above all, for He is the Head, the Sign, the Crown and the Wreath. The Word dwelleth in Him and Vision, fragrant perfume and the Ear which heareth all things. (*ATŠ*, p. 232, No. 114.)

[1] The name 'Mara-ḏ-Rabutha' is given to Adam Kasia in his aspect of Arch-priest and Initiator into the higher rites. A priest who initiates a novice is a *rba* (vulgar *rbai*) and the office of teacher to intending priests is called *rabutha*.

IX

THE LANGUAGE AND IDIOM OF NAṢIRUTHA

IN Western art, poetry, and rhetoric, personified abstractions such as Liberty, Truth, and Charity are often invoked: they are portrayed as asleep, smiling, weeping, betrayed, or victorious, but they are not worshipped. Gnosticism deliberately employed anthropomorphisms; it was no unconscious choice which evolved the Valentinian *Sophia* (Wisdom), the Marcosian *Ennoia* (Idea, Thought), and the Naṣoraean *Mana* (Mind). There had been ratiocination: the inventors of gnostic systems needed a fresh language to convey metaphysical concepts: they sought ways of conveying philosophical ideas in terms of religion and of expressing the belief that the material world was an illusion of the senses.

The process was a gradual one. It is difficult to detect where the language of poetry ends[1] and that of Jewish eclecticism begins, an eclecticism which gradually freed itself from Judaism and became gnosticism. We see the process at work in the pre-Christian Book of Enoch and the Wisdom of Solomon. In the latter, for instance, Wisdom 'is a breath of the power of God', 'an effulgence from everlasting light'; she 'hath power to do all things' and 'from generation to generation passing into holy souls she maketh men friends of God and prophets'.[2] Addressing God the poet says: '(Thou) who madest all things by thy Word and by thy Wisdom thou formedst man . . . give me Wisdom, her that sitteth by Thee on Thy throne.'[3] Such language, divorced from Judaism and wedded to syncretism, fathered gnosticism.

Philo and before him Aristobulus, both Alexandrian Jews,

[1] In Iranian religion there is a pantheon of deified abstractions such as Haurvatāt ('wholeness'), Amərətāt ('immortality'), &c.

[2] Wisd. of Sol. vii. 25, 26, 27.

[3] Ibid. ix. 1–4.

already stood half-way. Although both were loyal to the Jewish faith and customs of their fathers, they had imperceptibly reached a point at which Judaism could absorb a number of syncretistic theories; it was but a short step to the gnostic theology of the Naṣoraeans. Philo had already presented the macrocosm-microcosm idea, so prominent in Naṣirutha in a manner likely to appeal to Jew and Gentile alike: in the Book of Enoch the metaphysical Adam already appears. Gnostics of the earlier Naṣoraean school found, ready-made as it were for their purposes, such Old Testament figures as Adam (man),[1] Enoš (mankind), and Eve *Hawa* (Mandaic wind, breath, spirit).[2]

To these personified figures allegorical narratives were attached. The art of exegesis had been employed for a long while: Philo used it to reconcile Stoicism with Hebrew stories which he retold exegetically. *Haggadah* was the name given by Jews to this well-known way of telling and retelling stories in a way which conveyed hidden meaning. It was practised widely and not only by Jews of the Diaspora. Jesus taught in parables and some of the stories about Him related in the Gospels were thought by the scholarly Origen to be unhistorical.[3]

[1] The Qumran community must have believed in the other derivation of Adam, i.e. אָדם, 'red', for they constantly refer to his being made of dust, i.e. red earth, which refers to the 'physical' rather than the ideal Adam.

[2] In Mandaic *hawa* means both 'wind' and 'Eve'. Professor G. R. Driver writes to me: 'This resembles the Ass.-Bab. awû "to speak", Ugaritic *hwt* "voice" = Hebrew הֹוָה, הַוָּה *hōwāh, hawwāh* "bluster"; "ill-wind, ill luck"; "disaster" and Syriac ܗܘܬܐ "ruin" and ܗܘܐ "wind; disaster". The basic sense may be seen in Arabic هَوَى, "blew"; "whispered"; "rushed; fell". I presume that Hebrew הָיָה, הָוָא (= Aramaic הֲוָא) "fell (?), fell into, became, was" is the same root. Obviously this is an onomatopoeic root; "open your mouth", "expel the breath" (etc.). . . . Your main contention of *hawa* "breath, wind, spirit" seems to be incontestable.'

[3] Origen, *De Principiis* (of the gospels): '. . . those narratives which appear to be literally recorded there are inserted and interwoven, things which cannot be admitted historically, but which may be accepted in a spiritual signification'. St. Augustine is said to have adopted Christianity only when he learnt from Ambrosius that the Bible was to be understood allegorically rather than literally. According to Reinhold Merkelbach ('Eros u. Psyche', *Philologus* 102, 1958, p. 114), 'Dieser Art der Exegese stämmt aber aus ägyptischer Tradition und ist zum Beispiel von dem alexandrinischen Priester und Philosophen Chairemon geübt worden.'

Carrying symbolism further in order to conceal secret doctrine from the uninitiated, the gnostics invented a code-language of their own, to which Jewish mystics contributed *Gematria*, that assigned a number and hidden meaning to each letter of the alphabet. Finally the Pythagorean number-mysticism provided them with yet another method of mystification. Indeed, a searcher for the inner meaning of such literature is often reminded of the Russian doll which when pulled apart discloses another, and yet another, reaching finally the tiny inmost figure —itself an image!

The Naṣoraean availed himself of this language of symbol and occasionally himself furnishes a key. For instance, in *ATŠ* (p. 179, No. 236) he explains that by 'Adam and Eve', 'Ram and Rud', 'Šurbai and Šarhabiel',[1] 'Ether and Fire', 'Sun and Moon', he means 'soul and spirit'. Elsewhere 'soul and spirit' are likened to the primal cosmic Father and Mother, and the latter pair are reflected in a number of 'pairs and opposites', such as Sun and Moon, Radiance (*ziwa*) and Light (*nhura*), Sky and Earth, Rain and Earth, or Water and Earth, Date-palm and Well-spring, Gold and Silver. In this language of hidden meaning the tomb is a womb and the womb a tomb. 'Crossing the *yama ḏ-Suf*'[2] means crossing from a material state to the world of spirit.

It is sometimes possible to recognize code words in other gnostic systems. For instance, we are told of the Manichaeans,[3] that souls of the deceased (the sparks) are conveyed to the moon, which swells like a pregnant woman till the fifteenth night

[1] These are the names of surviving human pairs left to repeople the earth after the destruction by sword and plague, by fire and by water of its inhabitants, each pair, like Noah and his wife, being sole survivors. These periodic destructions, caused by astrological conditions, must be related to the Persian and Greek traditions of destructions by flood and fire at the 'great year', a time when the planets had moved to their original positions in the heavens in relation to the constellations of the Zodiac. The theory must have been Babylonian in origin, but was held by Plato, Pythagoras, and Aristotle (see B. L. van der Waerden, 'Das große Jahr u. die ewige Wiederkehr', *Hermes* 80, 1952, pp. 129 ff.).

[2] The Red or Reed Sea, 'Sea of the End'.

[3] F. Legge, *Forerunners and Rivals of Christianity* (Cambridge Univ. Press, 1915, 2 vols.), vol. ii, p. 308; also H. C. Puech, *Le Manichéisme*, p. 80.

when, purified by the sun, they rise by the 'column of glory' to perfection. The pattern is familiar: gestation in the womb of the 'Mother', birth, purification by the 'Father', and ascension in the *'ṣṭun* (see page 21, n. 1) to ultimate perfection—in the Naṣoraean idiom, ascent through the Mystic Adam to worlds of light. In short, we could have here reference to a Manichaean 'mystery' to assist the ascension of a departed soul.

Figures of speech used by Naṣoraeans are familiar to us in the Old and New Testaments: they are those which spring naturally to the lips of tillers of the soil who depend on mountain freshets as well as on perennial streams for water to irrigate field, garden, and vineyard and on rain to produce grazing for their flocks. In the Bible as well as in Naṣoraean literature the vine becomes the symbol of the whole community as well as that of the true believer.[1] The use of this simile is intensified in Mandaean poetry, the word *gufna*, 'a grape-bearing vine', is attached or added to the names of angelic beings as an honorific or title, e.g. Ayar-Gufna, Ruaz-Gufna, Šar-Gufna, &c. Yawar (*GR*r 321, ult.) is designated as 'the first Vine':

> Yawar, the great Radiance of Life,
> The First Vine (*gufna qadmaia*)
> Who is set (planted) on the earth
> Of the mighty First Life.

This and other similes[2] are unlikely to have originated in the present home of the Mandaean sect where the date harvest replaces the vintage of milder climes. In one hymn Carmel is mentioned:

[1] Hebrew גֶּפֶן, Akkadian *gupnu*.

> Vines shone in the water
> And in the Jordan they grew mighty.
> (*ML* 177.)

[2] The words of Jesus (John xv. 1 f.), 'I am the true vine and my Father is the husbandman', would be intelligible to Naṣoraeans in the sense implied, namely the claim to be the rightful 'vine' amongst other claimants to that term.

I ascended thee, Mount Carmel,
Thee I ascended, Mount Carmel.
Twelve vines awaited me:
They saw me, the vines beheld me!
When they saw me the vines waxed great,
Their foliage they spread out.

CP Prayer 212 describes the soul's ascent into the Vine:

There is a vine for Šitil and a tree for Anuš:
Šitil hath a vine yonder in thee, Land of the true,[1]
Laden with reward, laden with oblation
And laden with Naṣirutha.
The tendrils that curl at the leaf-ends
Bore prayers, hymns and sublime recitations.

When I arose in my place
I made a request that was great;
I asked that a tall ladder be given me
That I might place it against the Vine for ascent,
That against the Vine for ascent I might place it
And might mount into my Vine,
Might wax great and grasp its foliage,
Might eat, be refreshed by its shade
And enjoy its leafiness,
Might twine me a wreath of its tendrils
And place it upon my head.

Vines as true believers occur in the first of the baptismal hymns:

In the name of the Life
And in the name of Knowledge-of-Life
And in the name of that Primal Being
Who is Eldest and preceded Water,
Radiance and Glory; the Being who
Cried with His voice and uttered words.
Because of His voice vines grew and came into being
And the First Life was established in its abode.

Hearers are urged to uproot the bad vine and replace it by a good one (*GR*r 22, ult.). If vines droop and fail, they must be

[1] The inhabitants of Mšunia Kušṭa: the world of ideal counterparts.

uprooted (*GR*r 48: 15). In the *GR* the sacramental form used for the grape-bearing vine, *hamar-kana*[1], does not occur. As explained elsewhere, the sacramental wine is not fermented juice but water reddened by the maceration of grapes or raisins.[2] *Hamar-kana* has a further meaning, for *kana* means 'a group', 'an assemblage', as well as 'a root', hence the expression *kana ḏ-nišmata* (congregation or 'root' of souls) is linked by its double meaning to the vine just as in Ps. lxxx. 8 ff. the vine is used as a symbol of the people of Israel.[3]

Indeed the synoptics as well as the Fourth Gospel[4] abound in phrases and allusions understood and used by Naṣoraeans, such as 'children of light and children of darkness',[5] 'living water', 'everlasting life', 'bread of life', references to wheat and grain, sheep and shepherd, fish and fisherman, and so on. Names are 'blotted out of the scrolls' of divine beings; the Day of Judgement (*yum dina*) and the Last Day are constantly mentioned. There are those who have ears and do not hear. Souls stumble and are supported, stray from the right path, and there is the 'Way' which must be followed without diverging. All these expressions and similes occur over and over again in the Naṣoraean literature.

Ritual texts and commentaries use the words 'Seek and find,

[1] *Hamar*, status absolutus of *hamra*, 'wine'.

[2] In the *masiqta* the wine-cup represents the womb of the cosmic Mother in which the body of Adam Kasia is formed.

[3] Cf. the 'Vine of souls' in:

> Thou wilt rise up to the Place
> Which is the House of Perfection:
> Thou wilt wander freely in the Ether
> And wilt behold the sublime Vine of Souls
> In which sons of the great Family of Life
> Are represented. (*CP* 379.)

[4] Professor Dodd in his *Interpretation of the Fourth Gospel* (Cambridge Univ. Press, 1953), p. 411, has pointed out, in his discussion of the eucharistic aspect of the vine in that gospel, that in the Synoptic accounts of the Last Supper 'the contents of the cup are expressly described as γένημα τῆς ἀμπέλου, which is hardly a mere synonym for "wine"'. (Cf. Matt. xxvi. 29, &c., and Souter, *Lexicon NT*, svv. with definitions and cross-references.) Professor Bultmann (*Evangelium des Johannes*, Göttingen, 1950) has pointed out in great detail parallels with Mandaean phrases in the Fourth Gospel.

[5] The Qumran scrolls use this and other phrases common to Jewish literature of the period.

speak and be heard' as an initiation formula[1] (the corollary 'knock and it shall be opened to you', Luke xi. 9, does not follow). The equivalent of a 'voice from heaven' (בַּת קוֹל) is often heard in Mandaean narratives and a cry of woe on earth is heard and answered, especially in the magical texts. Naṣoraeans use some words which might be called 'parables in miniature'. Children and disciples are called 'plants': taking a wife (which is understood to imply founding a family) is 'planting a plant' or 'establishing propagation', for the word *niṣubta* both in Mandaic and Syriac has extended meanings such as 'procreation', 'fertilization', 'reproduction', and in such texts as the *ATŠ* it often means 'bride'.

There is no precise explanation of the symbolic meaning of myrtle, the presence of which is necessary to all Mandaic rites.[2] It may be that in some earlier form of the 'mysteries' myrtle was not originally a necessary adjunct, or it may perhaps have been because ritual inhalation (still practised by Jews, see *WW*) resembled too nearly Magian barsom-rite. In which case, reticence may be, like the silence on the subject of the sacred fire, due to the dangerous proximity of the Magians. The myrtle prayers, however, appear to be ancient. Myrtle is used in Jewish rites, and in my book *WW*, chap. vi, I described these and pointed out similarities with Parsi ceremonies. In *MMII* (p. 206) I said:

> The drinking of the *hamra* follows the *Abahatan*[3] and this drinking of fresh fruit juice and water is combined throughout with myrtle rites and the formal 'smelling the perfume of the myrtle', thereby intensifying . . . the implied symbolism of evergreen immortality and of the resurrection forces of spring, germination, and growth.

The wealth of symbolic phrases, of symbolic words, of symbolic acts of personification, and the use of the 'ear that hears and the eye that sees' make Naṣirutha, even in its most extravagant expression, the poetry of religion.

[1] For instance at ordination this phrase is said before the novice enters the cult-hut for the final coronation and investiture.

[2] The omission of myrtle and of the myrtle wreath is a sin, which according to *Mhita uasata* (*ATŠ*) needs purification by baptisms, repetition of the Rahmia (family office), and so on.

[3] The longer Commemoration prayer. *CP* 72, *ML*, p. 108, gives only the shortened version.

X

THE BAPTIZERS AND THE SECRET ADAM

It is with consciousness of temerity that I venture in this chapter to touch on subjects that are outside my own special ground of study. I ask, therefore, for forbearance in the hope that scholars better equipped than myself may find in the following attempt to trace the Naṣoraean Adam grounds for further study of early Jewish gnosticism.

In Chapter V I quoted from the Pseudo-Clementine Disputations. As remarked in a footnote to page 41, the dates of this romance and that of writings presumably used as its sources are still the subject of controversy. Nevertheless, it seems to be agreed that the Disputations reflect the opinions and beliefs of Jewish Christians between the first and fourth centuries,[1] and, as such, they must be treated as genuine. The fictional dispute between Peter and Simon the Magian, therefore, is of value to this inquiry of ours. It is represented as carried on in the Socratic tradition, with courtesy and logic on both sides.[2]

[1] See O. Cullmann, 'Die neuentdeckten Qumrantexte und das Judenchristentum der Pseudoklementinen', *Neutestamentliche Studien für Rudolf Bultmann*, Berlin, 1954.

[2] Simon, like Marcion, sees in the Jewish Creator a being who is often unjust, cruel, partial, and fallible, and, posing as a fundamentalist, he quotes the OT to prove it. He tells Peter that the Jewish Creator-God is really identical with the Demiurge who, indeed, was formed in the image of God as said in Genesis, but sprang in anthropomorphic form from a Supreme Being who is unknowable, ineffable, and entirely beyond human comprehension.

Peter defends the OT whilst accusing it of being the faulty work of man: if statements derogatory to God appear in it, they are not to be believed. 'Whatever sayings of the Scriptures are in harmony with the creation that was made by Him are true, but whatever are contrary to it are false' (*H.* III. xlii). Peter denies that Adam, 'who was fashioned by the hand of God', was 'a transgressor' (*H.* II. lii). It seems that Peter regards Adam as something more than the father of mankind, however, and he hints that Adam was reincarnated as Christ: 'but the Other, as Son of Man, being a Male, prophesies better things in the world to come' (*H.* III. xxii).

In spite of the defamation which gathered, understandably enough, about his name, Simon the Magian, arch-heretic and Samaritan, left an indelible impression not only on his contemporaries, as related in Acts viii, but on his successors, for he founded a school and heresy which long survived him. His Messianic claims were believed in by many; and although his miracles, or what passed as such, were branded as magic by his opponents, no doubt a *tu quoque* was not missing, although it has not survived.[1]

For an inquirer about Mandaean Naṣirutha the importance of Simon is shown by the fact that by Hippolytus and Eusebius as well as by the author of *H* this Magian is described as a baptist and as a disciple of John the Baptist. On both counts, this makes the Clementine picture of Simon a valuable one as representing a still surviving tradition about one who has been called 'the first Gnostic'. The chief point at issue between the disputants is not, as one might have expected if the original is a late one, the Messiahship or Sonship of Jesus, whom Peter calls 'this good king', 'the prophet of the Truth', 'the true prophet', one 'of a succession of prophets, being sons of the world and having knowledge of men'; it is the difference between Peter's view of Adam and his Creator and that of Simon. According to Peter, God the Creator first made the world and all that is in it, and then his creature Adam. Peter is a monotheist and defends his position as such, whereas Simon, according to Peter, is a polytheist who places another Unknown and Unknowable God above the Jewish God the Creator, and thus turns Jehovah into his Agent.

What actually was Simon's teaching? Hippolytus gives a somewhat confused account in book vi of his *Refutations of all Heresies*, using as his source Simon's own book *Great Announcement*, now lost. According to it, above this our world are great creative powers, 'from above', male in character, and 'from below' (female): he calls the first pair 'Mind' and 'Intelligence' (or 'Idea', *Ἔννοια*). These are the production of a 'Great Indefinite

[1] See A. D. Nock, *Conversion: from Alexander the Great to Augustine of Hippo* (Clarendon Press, 1933).

Power' 'at the root of all things'. He likens it to fire, which is of two kinds,[1] secret and manifest: the former may be perceived by the spiritual but 'evades the power of the senses'. The generated world springs from the 'Unbegotten Fire' that is from God (Deut. iv. 24).

> He who was begotten from the principle of that fire took six roots... primary ones of the originating principle of generation. And he says, that the roots were made from the fire in pairs, which roots he terms 'Mind' and 'Intelligence', 'Voice and Name', 'Ratiocination' and 'Reflection'.[2] (*Refutation, &c.*, A–N Library, bk. VI, chap. ix, p. 201.)

Simon's Tree of Life has yet another, seventh, root which permeates and dwells in the others: 'a great, indefinite, existing power' which is androgynous. Simon calls it 'the Father' and 'He who stood, stands, and will stand'.[3] This bisexual, creative power is the emanation of pre-existent, indefinite Being.[4] The All-Supreme, the 'One Root', is *Sige* (Silence), Invisible and Incomprehensible. It exists in isolation yet has expressed Itself in creative emanations 'in a state of duality'. Hippolytus sees in the mystical fire of Simon a plagiarism from Heraclitus, but we must not forget that Simon was called a Magian, and here we may see an effort to reconcile the Pentateuch to the sacred and purifying fire of the mobeds. The method of identification is

[1] In the Mandaean books we get constant reference to two kinds of fire, *'kilta* and *haita*, 'consuming' and 'living'.

[2] Cf. the Kabbalistic *Ḥokhmah* and *Binah*.

[3] We have here a possible mistranslation from the Aramaic. The Pa'el form of *QUM* [*qāim* (qayyim)] certainly means 'standing'. In Mandaic, in the Commemoration Prayer the words *ḏ-qaimia bpagraihun* mean 'who are living (alive) in their bodies'. In this sense the participle means 'living'; conversely 'lying down' and 'sleeping' are synonyms for death.

[4] Simon's Unknowable Cause of the universe and androgynous 'Father' creator of the world correspond in many respects to the Mandaean 'Great Life' and Adam Kasia. In the Simonian system, not only is the first Cause infinite but also, according to Hippolytus, a medial Space filled with 'air' (ether) without beginning or end. This corresponds nearly enough to the Mandaean ether-world and to the 'all-pervading air' taken as witness in the 'Epistle of Peter to James' in *H*. The authenticity of the latter is denied: but the tradition is interesting. Another parallel is the Pehlevi deity Vay (see *Zurvan*, p. 88), of which Zaehner says that it became 'identified with the Void or intermediate space between the realms of light and darkness . . . further identified with Space'.

truly gnostic, and habits of reasoning learnt in Greek (Alexandrian?) academies, mysticism in the dress of philosophy, lie behind Simon's doubtless sincere interpretation of what he thought the truth.

According to Clementine tradition the immediate successor to John the Baptist was another Samaritan, Dositheus, as Simon was in Egypt at the time of the Baptist's martyrdom. *H.* II. xxiv recounts that when Simon returned, the two men quarrelled. Simon's superiority was proved miraculously and Dositheus ceded his position as head of the sect to Simon. Legend may contain grains of truth and we know from patristic sources that baptizing sects of the Simonian school survived for some time. Eusebius in his *Ecclesiastical History*, IV. xi, names offshoots of the Simonian type: Simon's immediate successor, the Samaritan Menander (op. cit. III. xv), Saturninus in Antioch, and in Rome Cerdo, all came under this heading. The last-named, according to Eusebius, settled in Rome in the time of 'Hyginus who held the ninth place in the Apostolic succession'. Contemporary with Cerdo and Valentinus was Marcus, whose sacramental mysteries are described in a slanderous manner by Irenaeus.[1] In what appears to have been a *hieros gamos* rite, 'cups were mixed with wine'.[2] Eusebius gives a slightly more moderate account:

> Some of them [*i.e. the Marcosians*] construct a bride-chamber and celebrate a mystery with certain invocations on their initiate and say that what they do is a spiritual marriage according to the likeness of the unions above; others bring them to water and baptize them with this invocation; 'To the name of the Unknown Father of the Universe, to Truth, the mother of all things, to Him who descended into Jesus', and others invoke Hebrew words in order more fully to amaze the initiate. (Op. cit. IV. xi.)[3]

[1] Ag. Her. bk. I, xiii, A-N Library, vol. i, p. 51, and bk. I, xxi, 3, A-N Library, vol. i, p. 82.

[2] The mingling of water with wine retained its *hieros gamos* character in the Eastern churches (see *WW*, chap. 5). Mandaean commentaries on the rite of water into wine are explicit about its meaning, see pp. 79 f.

[3] Kirsopp Lake's translation, Loeb Library (Heinemann, 1943), vol. i, p. 329.

The words 'who descended into Jesus' recall the Jewish-Christian belief recorded in *H* that Jesus, as Messiah[1] and Son of God, had appeared in or been foreshadowed by other 'true prophets' or 'prophets of the truth'; a belief which appears plainly in Luke ix. 18–20, Matt. xvii. 10–13, and John i. 21.

That divine inspiration arises from an indwelling of the Celestial Adam is a fundamental tenet of the Elkasaite heresy. Simon the Magian, too, looked upon himself as an embodiment of, or as possessed by, the divine 'Father', the androgynous Father-and-Mother in One, when he calls himself 'the Standing (*i.e.* '*living*', '*persisting*') One'. Like the Simonian Adam, the Adam of the Elkasaites appears, as it were, at intervals as a divine intervention, recalling mankind to its spiritual source, the first spiritual Adam.

We hear first of the Elkasaite heresy in Hippolytus (*Refutation of all Heresies*, bk. IX, chap. viii, A–N Library, vol. i, p. 345). The eponymous founder of the sect, according to Hippolytus, was the 'false prophet' called *Ηλχασαι*. By Hippolytus and Fathers of the Church who subsequently wrote about this heretical sect 'Elkasai' was taken to be a man and author of a book. St. Augustine described him as 'the false prophet Elci' followed by the Sampsaeans and Elkasaites. Epiphanius spelt his name Elxai (*Ἤλξαι*) and calls the Elkasaites *Ἐλκασαίοι*. Origen has for the latter *Ἐλκασαιταί* and Theodoret talks of *Ἔλκασαι* as the founder of the sect. Much later, Elkasai reappears as Āl- Ḥasiḥ who, al-Nadīm asserts, is regarded by the Mughtasilah as their founder—and the Mughtasilah he identifies with the 'Ṣābians of the marshes'.[2]

Hippolytus, writing of the appearance of the sect of the Elka-

[1] The Messiah expected by first-century Jews was an anointed and crowned king of Israel according to T. H. Gaster, *The Scriptures of the Dead Sea Sect* (Secker & Warburg, 1957), p. 36.

[2] See D. Chwolsohn, *Die Ssabier und der Ssabismus* (St. Petersburg, 1856, 2 vols.), vol. ii, p. 542; Brandt (*Die jüdische Baptismen*, p. 109) writes: 'Nehmen wir die Identität des el-Ḥasaiḥ mit dem El-Khasai an, so ist es vor allem festzustellen daß das elchasäische Religionsbuch sehr wohl einmal zu den Baptisten am untern Euphrat den Weg gefunden und bei ihnen dann auch zu Ansehen gelangt sein kann. Ein anderer Zweig der Ṣabier des Qorân sind die mandäischen Baptisten . . . .'

saites in Rome during the second year of Hadrian's rule as emperor, says that a Syrian named Alcibiades—

> Brought some book alleging that a certain just man, Elchasai, had received this from Serae, a town in Parthia and that he gave it to one called Sobiaï (Σοβιαΐ). (Op. cit., bk. IX, chap. viii, A–N Library, vol. i, p. 345.)[1]

The book, Hippolytus continues, was revealed by an angel of gigantic proportions with whom was 'a female' of equal size. Those converted and obeying the book were to receive remission of sins by baptism. This baptism (op. cit., bk. IX, chap. x, A–N Library, vol. i, p. 348) needed witnesses, which Hippolytus names as 'heaven, water, holy spirits, angels of prayer, oil, salt and earth'.

Here there are parallelisms with the Mandaeans. They too invoke witnesses at baptism: they are *pihta* (bread made with salt), *mambuha* and the Jordan (i.e. the running water used for drinking and immersion), *Habšaba* (the personified first day of the week, Sunday) and *Zidqa* (oblation).[2] (See *CP* 21.)

[1] Miscomprehension of another language and a foreign alphabet can be traced here. 'Serae' may be, not a town, but a group of Jewish pietists of that name living in Parthia, the *Seres* (see *The Clementine Recognitions*, bk. VIII, xlviii (A-N Library, Clark, Edinburgh, 1867), p. 390), and, in spite of Brandt's doubts (*Elchasai*, p. 44), 'Sobiaï' probably stands for *Ṣubba* or Ṣabians, i.e. immersers, baptists. Transliteration of Aramaic into Greek constantly leads patristic writers astray; some Hebrew letters have no exact equivalent in the Greek alphabet (e.g. צ and כ). The various methods of transliterating the latter are exemplified in the various spellings of *Kasai* in Elkasai's name, and the first syllable, as is suggested on another page, is also rendered by various spellings. If I am right in supposing it to have been עֵיל, these are explained. Professor Driver agrees with me that the Ēl would be approximated by the *'Āl* (in Arabic), as both mean 'high', 'celestial' (עֵיל, 'high one', can be equated with עַל, 'the high god'). In O.-Ass. A-al-ṭâb = 'Al is good', I-li-a-lu-um = 'my god is Al(um)'. 'Obviously', he says, 'Elxai contains the Aramaic עֵיל, "high one", a title of God.'

See *Canaanite Myths and Legends*, ed. G. R. Driver (editor of the Ugaritic poems), Clark, Edinburgh, 1956, p. 54. *Kasai* for 'secret', 'mystic', 'hidden', is a W. Aramaic form. In the *GR* Jewish names usually end with *ai*, e.g. 'nišbai, Miriai, Šilai, Salbai, &c.

[2] Salt, according to the Drašia ḏ-Yahia (*JB* text, 166: 9 f.), 'is the mystery of the soul'. Its addition or omission when kneading the sacramental bread is symbolical. For baptism bread is salted, but the *faṭiria* which represent the dead are unsalted. Salt must be on the altar table for the *zidqa brika* (Blessed Oblation), the fifth of the witnesses quoted above (see *WW*, pp. 235–46).

The witnesses named by Hippolytus were invoked by the Elkasaites when, after being bitten by a rabid dog or other vermin, victims were bidden to immerse themselves immediately in running water, 'in their clothes'. After a similar mishap, Mandaeans, too, immerse themselves immediately, wearing the *rasta*, the white dress which, according to them, they formerly wore continually, like the Essenes. Moreover, should a Mandaean die from such a cause, a special *masiqta* called *Zihrun Raza Kasia* must be celebrated for the soul of the departed which is grievously polluted by such a death. Mandaeans, like Elkasaites (according to the heresiologists), must immerse themselves immediately after cohabitation, *pollutio noctis*, and possession by disease-demons.

To return to Hippolytus:

> And he [Elchasai] asserts that Christ was born a man in the same manner common to all and that he was not for the first time [on earth] born of a virgin but that both previously and frequently again he had been born and would be born: would thus appear and exist undergoing alterations of birth and having his soul transferred from body to body. (Op. cit., bk. IX, ix, A–N Library, vol. i, p. 347.)

The phrase 'born of a virgin' may have been an interpolation, for the virgin birth was always denied by Judaeo-Christians, but the rest agrees well with the idea of the periodical return of the 'true prophet'. Hippolytus mentions in a scornful manner their

> . . . formulae for those bitten by dogs, possessed by demons and seized by other diseases.[1]

By the second century, as shown by Hippolytus, the Elkasaite gnosis was sending out its missionaries. In the fourth its conquests were continued. According to Epiphanius, bishop of

In *H* bread and salt are consumed at the meal which follows baptism (*H*. XIV. i). At the Jewish Havdalah, bread is dipped into salt by orthodox Jews.

As for witnesses to an oath, see *H*, *Epistle of Peter to James*, p. 3: the initiate swears—or promises, since oaths are forbidden to a Jew—by heaven, earth, water, and air ('the all-pervading ether') and the formula is to be repeated whilst standing in running (living) water.

[1] Up to the present day exorcisms of disease and lunacy-demons form part of the library of every Mandaean priest.

Salamis in Cyprus who wrote about the heresy some hundred and fifty years later, it had won adherents beyond Jordan, the Dead Sea, and in Nabaṭaea. Among its converts, he tells us, were Ebionites, Nazarenes, Ossaeans (probably Essenes), Nasaraeans (with a sigma), and Sampsaeans. The Ebionites (*ebionim*)[1] were the Judaeo-Christians who were classed with heretics by the now dominant catholicized Pauline church. The Judaeo-Christians were divided in observance and belief: some continued to circumcize and observe the Sabbath and some not. Some, following the example of James the brother of Jesus,[2] were vegetarians and ate no meat. Blood-sacrifice, since the destruction of the Temple, was dead: it had been frowned upon by the Essenes and others before them. Baptizing Jews thought that the sacrament of baptism replaced it. The Ebionites for the most part had settled in Transjordania.

As for the sect or sects which he calls Nazarenes or Naṣoraeans[3] (spelling the word in several manners) he distinguishes

[1] *Ebionim* ('poor ones') was originally a term of praise, not contumely, as later. They may have been the 'poor in spirit' of whom Jesus spoke. See Eusebius, *Ecc. Hist.* III. xxvii.

[2] According to Hegesippus, who lived about a generation and a half after James's martyrdom, which he described (see Eusebius, *Ecc. Hist.* II. xxiii). His evidence is valuable as giving a picture of the followers of Jesus soon after his death. Of James he says that some inquired of him what was 'the gate of Jesus' and he replied that he was the Saviour. Owing to this answer, says Hegesippus, some believed that Jesus was the Christ (II. xxiii). He records that in Jerusalem some did not believe either in resurrection 'or in one who will come to reward each according to his deeds; but as many as believed did so because of James'.

Hegesippus says that James wore long hair, unshaven beard, linen clothing, and was a vegetarian. He did not anoint himself with oil, drank no wine, and did not visit the baths. This has been taken to mean that James was a Nazarite, but had he been, it is probable that Hegesippus would have said so. The Essenes (see Hieronymus, *Against Jovinian*, vol. ii, p. 14; *Nicene and Post-Nicene Fathers of the Christian Church* (Oxford, 1893), vol. vi, p. 397) also practised such austerities.

[3] Brandt (*Elchasai*, p. 53) notes the manner in which transliteration from Hebrew characters bedevils the word variously transliterated as 'Naṣoraean', 'Nazarene', 'Nazarite', &c. The last word with 'z'—Hebrew ז— as its middle consonant has an entirely different meaning from words derived from NṢR. NZR נָזַר, 'to separate, dedicate, vow oneself', seems to apply to ascetics who took a temporary vow not to cut their hair, drink wine, &c., at the end of which they cut their hair again. The exact meaning of נצר was discussed

them from the Judaeo-Christians, but leaves no clear picture of their differences from the Ebionites, but he does say of the latter (*Haer*. xxix. 6) that the first Christians 'did not call themselves Nasaraeans for the Nasaraean heresy was before Christ and knew not Christ'.

Epiphanius did not content himself with mere hearsay: he took trouble to find out from converts (he himself was a convert from Judaism) the Elkasaite point of view. Their Christ, according to him, was a *δύναμις*:

> Some of them, too, say that Christ is Adam, the first-created (being) . . . others say that he was created before all things, superior to the angels, ruling over all and called Christ.
>
> [He] put on the body of Adam, appeared as a human being, was crucified, arose and went up to Heaven.[1]
>
> Others say . . . but there came into him the Spirit which is Christ and put on the (human) nature which is Jesus.
>
> Christ was created in heaven and the Holy Spirit also—Christ first indwelt in Adam and from time to time withdraws from Adam and *parousia* takes place through incarnation.

Elkasaites such as these were probably Ebionites for whom the docetic theory explained the mystery of the shameful death of Jesus.

Other Elkasaites were not Christians. The Sampsaeans (*Σαμψαῖοι*)[2] were monotheists but not Christians or Jews or Greeks. Hence the Adam-figure was not the Christian Messiah. They declared the canonical books of the Christians to be falsified and dispensed with the Old Testament.

on p. xiv. Philologists and theologians for the most part (e.g. Schoeps, Torrey, and Burkitt) have decided that the form used in Matt. ii. 23 (*Ναζωραῖος*) could not mean 'of Nazareth'. In the Greek New Testament Jesus is *Ναζωραῖος* and *Ναζάρηνος*. In the Talmud he is referred to as נוצרי, *Nuṣri*. In Arabic 'Christians' are Naṣāra.

[1] For the Docetic heresy and an account of the opposition to it of Irenaeus and other ante-Nicene theologians, see Dr. J. N. D. Kelly, *Early Christian Doctrines* (A. & C. Black, 1958), pp. 141 ff.

[2] *Haer*. liii. 1. Jerome gave a similar report about some Nazarenes in a letter to Augustine.

These Sampsaeans were baptists: they honoured water and said that life had its origin in water. They too had a book which he was told was called '*Yexai*' after 'Elxai's brother' (*sic*)! However, he managed to see this book or a page or so of it, for he transcribed from it the following words:

אנא מסהד עליכון ביום דינא רבא

I will be your witness on the great Day of Judgement.

These words would, to a Mandaean, sound like a quotation from the Ginza (the 'Book of Adam' is its other name). In it there are many references to 'the great day of Judgement', 'the day of Judgement, the Hour of Deliverance'. In one such passage the Great Life addresses Adam:

Then spoke the Great First Life to Adam, Head of the Race [of mankind]. 'O Adam, rest at ease in thy glory: let the calm of the good come upon thee. Hibil-Ziwa is here, thy brethren the 'uthras are here and the Jordan; it is all here.

Here wilt thou dwell, Adam! Thy spouse Hawa is coming hither. Thy whole race will rise upward following after thee. This is the Abode prepared for thee, Adam, and thy spouse Hawa, in the presence of the Great Life until the Day, the Day of Judgement, the Hour of hours—of Deliverance, until the great Day of Uprising. Then, Adam, thou wilt rise upward and all thy race and wilt go to thine own world. Calm thy vigilance and let thy heart be reassured. (*GR*l 18 f.)

Like the Mandaeans and Ebionites, the Sampsaeans favoured early marriage and thought ill of celibacy. Epiphanius says of both Sampsaeans[1] and Ossaeans (Essenes?) that they had fallen away from Judaism and adhered to the Elkasaite heresy.

I have mentioned details in which the Elkasaite sects and Mandaean Naṣoraeans resemble one another. There is a much deeper ground for thinking that there is a common background and for believing that the Elkasaites were once closely related to our Naṣoraeans. The central cult of both is the Heavenly Man,

[1] The word 'Sampsaean' Epiphanius translated as 'sunny'. Perhaps the sect honoured the sun as symbolical in its setting and rising of death and resurrection. Traces of such symbolism still linger in the mass rites of the Eastern churches (see *WW*, pp. 143 and 218, n. 1). Šams شمس, = 'sun'.

Adam. In the secret scrolls the 'false prophet' of the Elkasaites can be recognized as the Naṣoraean Adam Kasia—no 'man' but Man, Anthropos, the Son of Man, the Son of God; El Kasia.[1] In his lower aspect he is the Demiurge, creator of 'worlds of illusion, seven to his right and seven to his left'. In his higher and divine aspect he is Mankind anointed and crowned, priest and king, an image of divine kingship. Above all, he is a sacramental symbol of union and resurrection: through the mystic recreation of his cosmic body, the departed soul receives its spiritual body. There are several difficulties in opposition to the identification.

To avoid confusion the Mandaean Naṣoraeans will be referred to as 'Naṣoraeans (M)'. If the original sacraments and cult of Naṣoraeans (M) can be traced back to as early a sect as that of the Elkasaites, how has it happened that the prefix 'El' has disappeared? Secondly, why was the Elkasaite belief that the Secret Adam reappeared from time to time as a prophet or as a crowned and anointed king abandoned by Naṣoraeans (M)? Were the original Naṣoraeans (M) Jews, or Samaritans, or what? Was their original home Judaea, or Samaria or Galilee, or did the cult start amongst Parthian Jews on the great trade route? At what period did the 'three hundred and sixty *tarmidia* (disciples) who came forth from the city of Jerusalem', commemorated in the longer *Ṭab ṭabia* prayer, leave that city? Why should the Naṣoraeans (M) hate the Jews so fiercely? Why, if Jews, did they give up circumcision, and when?

[1] Epiphanius's explanation of the first syllable as חיל, 'strength', 'power', has been accepted by some scholars with the result that they get 'secret Power' from Elkasai, e.g. H. J. Schonfield, *Secrets of the Dead Sea Scrolls* (Valentine, 1956), p. 122. Brandt had already considered this possible meaning, but was inclined to reject it (*Die jüdischen Baptismen*, p. 109). For the derivation suggested here, see p. 93, n. 1. In the Ras Shamra texts Adam is the son of *El*, which makes the possibility that 'El' here is עיל even more likely. Chwolsohn (*Die Ssabier.*, vol. i, pp. 116 ff.) connected the Elkasaites with the Mandaeans but did not associate the 'founder' of that sect with the Secret Adam, for Mandaean literature in his time was largely unread. He dwelt upon the fame of the Elkasaites as foretellers of the future, a reputation which they shared with the Essenes (see Josephus, *The Antiquities of the Jews* (Whiston, Edinburgh, n.d.), XVII. xiii. 3). The Mandaean priesthood is famous for the same reason; see the *Book of the Zodiac* (Royal Asiatic Society, London, 1949).

These are grave objections, and satisfactory answers to such questions should be found before the identity of Adam Kasia with Elkasai is proved.

The historical background, dim though it is, can help a little. The Parthian Empire at its height was far flung. During its long and successful appearance on the stage of the civilized world Jewish colonies were to be found in all the larger cities along the great trade routes. Many of them had been established long before: in Babylonia we have records of Jewish banking under Nebuchadnezzar. At the end of the 'Captivity' only a minority of Babylonian Jews returned to Palestine, and under the tolerant rule of the Achaemenids and Arsacids the Jews flourished. From one trading centre to another, from India to the Mediterranean, and from far China to the Persian Gulf, Jewish merchants travelled, tarried, and intermarried. For the most part they carried with them a tendency to monotheism or at any rate fidelity to their tribal god Yahweh. Well-to-do colonies sheltered Jewish academies and synagogues, where there was discussion and opportunity to satisfy that intellectual curiosity which has always been characteristic of the Hebrew. Alexandria was a seat of learning and had a large Jewish population. There, Greek thought and Oriental cults met and flourished: the Hermetic treatises which purported to be Egyptian were probably composed there and from this centre alone a stream of liberal and intellectual mysticism flowed out into the Mediterranean world of culture. Judaism held its own, but profited by its surroundings. Philo was no exception: others, such men as Aristobulus the philosopher, had preceded him. The age of syncretism had arrived and, as carriers from city to city, Jews must have contributed much towards this tolerant attitude toward the religion of others.

Dr. R. Ghirshman writes:[1]

> Under the Parthians there was a great expansion of Judaism in Babylonia. In 20 B.C. a small Jewish vassal state was established on the banks of the Euphrates and remained in existence nearly twenty

[1] R. Ghirshman, *Iran* (Pelican Books, 1954), p. 272.

years. The moral and intellectual life of the Jewish nation with its flourishing schools became centred in this area, in Babylon and the Greek cities, and played a part in the influence exercised by Jewish ideas on Iranian religion. During the great Jewish revolt of the second century A.D. which set all the Roman Orient ablaze, the rebels received aid from the Parthians, a fact which gave rise to the well-known saying: 'When you see a Parthian charger tied up to a tomb-stone in Palestine, the hour of the Messiah will be near.'

If the influence of Parthians and Greeks[1] over Judaism resulted in a certain fusion of ideas, there was reciprocity: Judaism had much to give as well as to take. Palestine was open on every side to foreign influence, yet preserved its individuality; Judaea remained very Jewish. What of Samaria and Galilee?

The Samaritans, as Josephus notes sourly more than once, were always glad to claim kinship with the Medes and Parthians near their borders to their own advantage when Jewish fortunes were low (*Antiquities*, x. ix. 7). Samaritans were usually ready to assist the enemies of the Jews, and though they cherished the Pentateuch they retained religious independence. In constantly close and friendly touch with Media and Parthia on the one hand and with Greek settlements on the other, Graeco-Iranian ideas, and, above all, those of the Magians must have had great influence over many of them. In Samaria, therefore, we have a natural forcing-bed for early gnosticism and it is significant that Simon called 'the Magian', Dositheus, and Simon's successor Menander were all Samaritans—and baptists.

What kind of a religion was professed in Media and Parthia during the era of Parthian domination? Dr. Ghirshman (op. cit. p. 268) writes: 'The Parthians were no more Zoroastrian than were the Achaemenians', and 'there is no great certainty what the state religion, if one existed, was'. That there was a fire-cult was probable.

If we assume tentatively that a form of gnosticism coloured by the Pentateuch could have appeared in Samaria or Parthia in the first century, perhaps even earlier; such a sect could, with

[1] For analysis of the Hellenic influence see Hans Jonas, *The Gnostic Religion* (Beacon Press, 1958), pp. 17 ff.

equal probability, have gained adherents in Galilee, which was separated from Judaea by Samaria. It might be in Galilee that our original Naṣoraeans (M) are to be sought and Epiphanius may be stating a truth when he says that there were 'Nasaraeans' in pre-Christian times, meaning, groups of dissident Jews whose teaching was not revealed to those who might decry its unorthodoxy and who perhaps celebrated 'mysteries' to which outsiders were not admitted. It may have been a form of 'Elkasaitism', i.e. mysticism centred about the figure of Divine Man.

Was John the Baptist connected with these? He left no book behind him, but there are traces of grave differences between his disciples and those of Jesus. It is certain that Simon the Magian was never a Naṣoraean (M) although the Divine Man was the centrepiece of his system, and he himself claimed to be a Messiah. Had he been, we might have found his name, like that of John the Baptist, in the Naṣoraean Commemoration prayer.[1] As remarked earlier in this book, John is never the mouthpiece of Naṣoraean doctrine as it appears in the secret scrolls, and John's figure may have been inserted at a later date, for the name *Yahia* is Arabic not Aramaic.

The figure of Adam in Canaan is an ancient one, and is bound to the Canaanite god at a very early time.[2] He was the son of 'El, so that it is natural to find him in the 'El-Kasai gnosis.[3]

The Naṣoraean connexion with Samaritan schools of thought would be enough to account for their detestation of the Jews,

[1] Although there is a legendary 'life' of John the Baptist in the *Haran Gawaita*, and he appears in both the *Ginza* and Drašia ḏ-Yahia, he is never represented as an incarnation of Adam as Son of Man, or as the founder of the religion. He is a baptist, a priest performing the priestly duty of a true Naṣoraean, and in *JB* he is a preacher. Worship of saints or the cult of holy men is wholly foreign to the whole temperament of Naṣirutha.

[2] See Ivan Engnell, *Studies in Divine Kingship in the Ancient Near East* (Almquist, Uppsala, 1943), p. 177.

[3] Adam as King-Priest: 'The connexion between Primordial Man and the actual ruler for this reason cannot be doubted and therefore the mythical conception of paradise and Primaeval Man has played a considerable role in royal ideology, the kind being as it were the Son of God, just because he is the representative of Primordial Man.' G. Widengren, 'Early Hebrew Myths and their Interpretation', in *Myth, Ritual and Kingship*, p. 175.

and for the manner in which they eradicated words which to them meant Jewry, such as the words *'El*, *Šaddai*, *mšiha*, and *Adonai*:[1] the hatred and opposition must have been mutual. Mandaean hatred for Christians, less pronounced than their hostility to Jews, is chiefly concentrated upon Jesus as Messiah. To the true Naṣoraean Adam could never be anything but a spiritual figure, an ideal humanity personified in Adakas, the earthly Adam's guardian, his soul, teacher, 'the Radiance which came from the Secret Place', the heavenly High Priest and King, of whom every earthly priest must be the crowned symbol. Hence the idea prevalent in Judaeo-Christian and in some Elkasaite circles that there was reincarnation of the Adam-Christ, if it had ever existed in Naṣoraean (M) gnosis, early disappeared, just as it did from Christianity. For Paul, Jesus was 'the Last Adam'.[2] Amongst the Judaeo-Christians and the Simonians in Rome the idea lingered awhile, but these heretical gnostics disappeared after a time.

Principles which, according to Epiphanius, were held by some adherents to Elkasaite gnosis, such as circumcision, food taboo, and observance of the Sabbath, do not appear in

[1] References in the *Ginza* and liturgical prayers show that Naṣoraeans (M) associated the word *'El* עיל and *Adonai* with Judaism. 'Praise not the sun, whose name is Adonai, whose name is Qadoš, whose name is *'El'El* (עיל עיל); moreover he hath secret names not revealed in this world' (*GR*r 24: 15 ff.). In the same book (*GR*r 455: 12) *'El* is again identified with Adonai and the sun. In the liturgical prayers (*CP* 75 = *ML* 127: 11 f.):

> Spirit (*ruha*) lifted up her voice;
> She cried aloud and said 'My Father, my Father!
> Why didst Thou create me? My god *'El 'El*,
> Why hast thou set me far away, cut me off,
> Left me in the depths of the earth
> And in the nether gloom of darkness
> So that I have no strength to rise up thither?'

The complaints of Sophia in the Valentinian Christian-Gnostic fragment are similar to this. Lines 3–4 above are

עיל עיל למאחו שאבאקתאן

which is possibly a variant of Psalm xxii. 1 and of the cry of Jesus on the cross (Matt. xxvii. 46; Mark xv. 34).

[2] See W. D. Davies, *Paul and Rabbinic Judaism*, p. 51.

Naṣirutha (M); which was not Judaic from the start. In Gentile Christian circles they faded away at once although they lingered in Judaeo-Christian communities.[1] Circumcision is abhorrent to Naṣirutha because to mutilate the human body is to mutilate that which was made in the image of God, and a man who has any imperfection in his sexual organs is unfit to be a priest.

We must leap over some centuries in the search for Primordial Man as he appeared to Magians. Amongst Magian sects described by the scholarly Shahrastānī in his *Kitabu-l Milal wal Nihal* was one which he calls the Kaiumartīya, worshippers of Kaiumart (i.e. the Avestan Gayomard or Gayomart, 'Life-Man'). He says of them:

> The Kayumartaeans say that Kaiumart was Adam, in the chronologies of the Indians and Persians, Kayumart.

Under the same heading *Majūs*, Magians, Shahrastānī mentions the influence of the Israelites which, he says, extended over Syria and westward beyond it, adding that it spread little to Persian countries (بِلَاد العجم). He continues:

> In the time of Abraham the Friend of God, the Parthians corresponded to two classes, one of them being the Ṣābians [Ṣābiya] and the other the Ḥanefites. And the Ṣābians said, 'For understanding the most High God, knowledge of and obedience to Him and His commandments and ordinances, a Mediator is necessary, but that Mediator must be a spiritual being and not of corporeal nature. This is so because of the purity of spiritual beings and their undefiled nature and because they are near to the Lord of lords; whereas Corporeality of Flesh resembles us, eating of all that we eat and drinking all that we drink and like us in matter and form.'

The 'spiritual Mediator' and 'Corporeality of Flesh' correspond to Adakas-Ziwa and to Adam Pagria. Shahrastānī's reference to the spread of Jewish influence shows that he was conscious

[1] It was Paul who threw open 'the gate of Jesus' to Gentiles, and it cost him a struggle to part with such ingrained Jewish principles as circumcision and food taboos, whereas Naṣoraeans (M), many of whom were probably of mixed race, with Greek and Parthian mysticism all about them, even in inherited tradition, had little to hold them to such customs even if, at one time or other, they had practised them.

of the manner in which Jewish and Iranian culture and religion had interacted upon one another—at a time when both were saturated also with Greek philosophy. The element which appears in an amazingly conservative form is that of Primordial Man, who, already in Canaanite times, was conceived of as King, Priest, and Son of God.

Every Mandaean priest is anointed, crowned, and given the insignia of kingship when he is ordained, for he is the earthly representative of the Heavenly Man: and every baptized person in anticipation of his union (*laufa*) with the redeemed body of the elect is taken, as it were, into the Body of Adam by a 'signing' with water and 'crowning' with a myrtle wreath, ceremonies repeated in his dying hour with the difference that the signing is with oil; for, as a true believer dying in purity, he will become one with the spiritualized humanity called the Secret Adam.

There is a unity in this which can be understood only by examining the Mandaean sacraments as symbolic of progression into the life to come and interpreting them by the secret teaching.

How did the severance between exoteric and esoteric teaching arise? The answer cannot be merely that 'mysteries' are always protected by secrecy in gnostic sects and mystery religions. There is a definite cleavage which must be explained.

I fear that nothing but speculation can provide an answer. As we know, the *Haran Gawaita*, which cannot be altogether dismissed as legend, relates how the Naṣoraeans fled from Jewish persecution to Media and Harran, and, later on, under the protection of Parthian rulers, into Lower Babylonia. What did these immigrants find on arrival?

Ritual immersion was ancient indeed in Babylonia, and during Iranian domination shrines had been built on the Tigris and Euphrates to the water-goddess Anahita,[1] who under her Semitic name Nanai or Nanaia is still invoked in Mandaean exorcism

[1] 'Artaxerxes II set up images of Anahita in Babylon, Susa, Ecbatana and established the cult in Persia, Bactria, Damascus, and Sardis' (A. D. Nock, *Conversion*, p. 355).

books.[1] Did these Naṣoraeans from Harran and Media find on the rivers of southern Mesopotamia and Khūzistān a baptizing sect so similar to their own that they incorporated and dominated it?[2] Guesswork should have no place in serious research, but we have yet to account for the curious fact that parts of books to which laymen have access are at variance with the secret doctrine, that Mandaeans as laymen are graded beneath the hereditary priesthood, and that even within that priesthood only a select few are admitted into the arcana of Naṣirutha, into the mystery of the Hidden Adam.

To sum up this mystery once again: the Hidden or Secret Adam is an emanation from the Great Life which appeared in the shape of Man and of material man who appeared later on earth. In his highest aspect, Adakas-Ziwa, the mystic Light-Adam, he is re-created at every *masiqta*, for he represents sublimated humanity, a state into which the souls of the departed who no longer 'stand in the body' pass after they have been provided by his re-creation with a new and spiritual body. In and by him they pass upward into 'worlds of light' and eventually, with him, into the final union with the Absolute which is above human imagination.

Although as 'soul' he exists in every man, he is, as we have

[1] See part iii of E. S. Drower, 'A Mandaean Book of Black Magic', *J.R.A.S.*, 1943, p. 159, and unpublished magical texts.

[2] In the long lists of copyists in colophons of the older sacred books we find at the end of most of them 'Ramuia son of 'Qaimat', 'Bainai son of Haiuna', and 'Zazai ḏ-Gawazta', men credited with the collection and editing of Mandaean manuscripts early in the Moslem era. They lived at al-Ṭīb, which was then the seat of a Mandaean ethnarch (*rišama*). This town, now non-existent, was situated between Wāsiṭ and Khūzistān. Yāqūt ibn 'Abdallāh al-Ḥamawī described it in his *Mu'ajjam al-Buldān* as 'one of the residences of Seth son of Adam'. Until they embraced Islam the inhabitants 'never ceased to confess the religion of Seth' and were of the Ṣābian faith. By describing them as 'Nabaṭaeans who spoke Nabaṭaean' he certainly indicated that they were of foreign descent who spoke an Aramaic not of the Babylonian type, for in the twelfth century in which he wrote there must still have remained many who still spoke Aramaic: in fact, there are still pockets of Aramaic-speaking people in 'Iraq. If, as Epiphanius stated, the Elkasaite doctrines spread into Nabaṭaea, the story in the *Haran Gawaita* that Naṣoraeans emigrated under Parthian protection into the marshes of Babylonia from the north-east becomes very credible (see *Mu'ajjam al-Buldān*, vol. vi, p. 76 (Cairo, 1906)).

shown by some extracts from the secret scrolls, recognized as king and priest. When the celebrant, breaking off fragments from the loaves before him which represent human souls, adds these to the *pihta* he holds to represent the newly departed, he does this to symbolize *Laufa*, that is, unity in this world and the next. When he crowns the *pihta* with a myrtle wreath and anoints it with *miša*, he indicates that the Secret Adam is a Messiah in the ancient sense of the word, a crowned and anointed king. He is Humanity fulfilled, ruler and victor.

EPILOGUE

RITUAL observances which concern cleanness and uncleanness described in the OT and those which appear in the later Jewish *Šulḥan 'Arukh* should be compared with similar and equally strict rules governing ritual purity in the Mandaean book *Mhita uasuta* and the Parsi regulations enumerated by Modi in his book on Parsi customs and usages.[1] The Naṣoraean observances are close to the latter, although the methods of cleansing ritual faults and impurities differ widely. Like the Parsi priest a Mandaean must avoid contact with dead matter, and should such a pollution occur it must be cleansed by baptism and *masiqtas*. Contact with any unclean thing or person debars a Mandaean priest from taking part in any rite: fear of touching a corpse is the reason why a Mandaean priest is forbidden to open his door to a dying person. This is one reason why an official go-between must be present at all rites. He acts as it were as a bridge between the laity and priests, and shields them from danger of pollution. I refer to the *ašganda*, whose office in some ways resembles that of a Christian deacon.

At a baptism the *ašganda* takes no part in the rite itself except at the beginning and end when he exchanges the ritual hand-clasp with the priest which expresses a form of oath or covenant. This ceremony takes place at every rite, and each time afresh the *ašganda* goes through a preliminary purification and consecration. The words of initiation which begin 'Seek and find, speak and be heard' are dictated to him. In the *masiqta* the *ašganda* is allowed to enter the cult-hut into which he takes the 'outer phial' when it is required. He must be of priestly birth and priests have usually had experience as *ašgandas* before they are 'crowned'.

In spite of all this care to preserve ritual 'cleanness', of laws rigorously observed for centuries, this very faithfulness to

[1] Modi, *The Religious Ceremonies and Customs of the Parsees.*

regulations of ritual purity is bringing doom upon the priestly caste. During an outbreak of cholera or plague during the early nineteenth century a great number of Mandaeans in Mesopotamia and Persia died. Constantly drinking infected water, and entering it with sick and dying persons, the entire priesthood perished. Not a single priest escaped. There was no one to baptize, to perform marriages, or to celebrate the last rites for the dying. Colophons to manuscripts copied at that time record that in desperation and with tears and misgivings a small group of survivors of priestly families who had formerly assisted as *ašgandas*, and thus knew most of the baptismal prayers by heart, assembled and agreed to consecrate one of their number as priest, performing the rites of consecration as best they could. Aided by anxious perusal of ritual scrolls, they set about the task of rebuilding the priesthood. The first new priest, therefore, had no qualified instructor and no proper initiation.

A new hierarchy was painfully built up. The sect, however, had suffered a blow from which it has never recovered and modern education and the impact of a Westernized, mechanized world is quickly completing the process of dissolution. In my own lifetime I have watched the approach of the end. In spite of one or two devoted priests, at baptismal feasts nowadays only the very young and very old come forward for baptism. The sons of *ganzibria* and priests enter lay professions and not the priesthood and, like the Mandaean laity who long ago ignored the old taboo, they cut their hair and dress like their neighbours.

At birth, marriage, and death a handful of priests still function, but they are nearly all aged men for whom there will be no replacement when they die. Yet, so strong is tradition, that it is likely that immersion and certain rites and customs will persist in some form or other even after the religion itself is dead. How strong such traditions are was brought home to me when, a few years ago, I returned to visit ʿIraq.

Whilst myself a patient in an American mission hospital at ʿAmarah, I was told that a Mandaean lad had been brought in from a marsh village. He was desperately ill: long-neglected bilharzia had reduced him to the point of death. The doctor examined him and told his father that the boy, his only son, was so ill that recovery was doubtful, but that they would accept him as a patient and give him treatment. The father realized that the balance was tipped towards death and wished to take the boy back with him, but the medical staff dissuaded him.

The next morning at breakfast I was told that the father had returned before dawn with a priest and a man who have must been an *ašganda*. In spite of protests by the night-nurse, the sick boy had been dressed in his *rasta* and carried down into the garden which is only a few yards from the river Tigris. There, they emptied three buckets of river water one after the other over the boy, who died there and then of the shock.

It fell to me to explain when the father and his friends asked to be allowed 'to build something' outside the door through which the corpse was to be taken out that morning for burial. The 'something' was the *mandelta*, a low row of three reed bundles over which the four bier-bearers must step and which, they said, must remain *in situ* for three days. Permission was eventually granted on an understanding that the hospital could not be responsible if hostile spectators or callers injured or removed the bundles. In reply, the Mandaeans said that they would guard it day and night.

Before noon, bier-carriers wearing white religious dress arrived: the corpse was carried out over the *mandelta* which the priest sealed with his iron ring (see *MMII*, pp. 181–4). An old man sat and lay by the reed bundles and kept watch until the third day after death, when they were removed.

The family was satisfied. The rites for the dying, the 'Letter', had, thanks to the presence of a priest in the town and the foresight of the father, taken place in time and no *Ahaba d̠-Mania*[1] would be necessary to redeem the boy's soul that year at Panja, (*Parwanaiia*) the 'five days of light' during which all the dead are remembered. And the dead boy's name would be called out

[1] See p. 51 and *MMII*, pp. 214–22.

in commemoration prayers with the names of others who had died during the previous year, with the customary phrase which pleads for forgiveness:

> Forgive him and them their sins, trespasses, follies, stumblings, and mistakes.

APPENDIX

IN a scholarly tome, *Die Ssabier und das Ssabismus*, published in 1856, the Russian scholar Dr. D. Chwolsohn assembled material gathered from Arab, Persian, and Jewish writings of the early Moslem epoch about the Ṣābians. Quoting a story told by the Christian Abū-Yūsuf Absaa' al-Qāṭī'i, he deduced that pagans who still worshipped gods of classical antiquity adopted the name as a cloak in order to acquire the protection promised by the Qur'ān to Jews, Christians, and Ṣābians as 'people of a book', for the Caliph Mamūn had told them that unless they chose to profess one of the tolerated religions they must become Moslems or die.

The erroneous identification of these pretended and pagan 'Ṣābians' with the real Ṣābians, who were according to Chwolsohn, 'low, ignorant Mandaeans of the marshes of 'Irāq', is the main theme of his erudite book. How could those poor ignorant Mandaeans be confused with the learned and famous Harranian pseudo-Ṣābians who did so much to bring Western philosophy, medicine, and astronomy to Moslems in Baghdad during the ninth, tenth, and early eleventh centuries? Nevertheless, these men did not become Moslems but continued to call themselves Ṣābians.

According to Shahrastānī's account of them in the Kitāb-al-Millal and that of Al-Kindī and other writers, the Harranian Ṣābians satisfied inquiry as to the nature of their religion with answers based upon Neo-Platonic philosophy rather than theology. Their references to Biblical figures such as Noah, Seth, and Anuš were, Chwolsohn suggested, thrown in as a sop to Moslem hearers, and their assertions that theirs was the religion of Agathodaemon and Hermes proved both their paganism and their learning.

That such brilliant scholars as the Ṣābian Thābit-ibn-Qurrah and his school, who were responsible for many translations into Arabic from the Greek, were acquainted with Stoic, Hermetic, and Platonic literature is of course probable;[1] nevertheless they may have been no pseudo-Ṣābians but genuine members of that sect, Naṣoraeans, who

[1] The Oxford scholar Walter Scott, in his *Hermetica* (Clarendon Press, 1924), followed Chwolsohn's argument closely, and took Harranian Ṣābian references to Hermes, Thoth, and so on as so much evidence that they were steeped in knowledge of Greek and Latin writings assigned to 'Hermes Trismegistus', the thrice-holy Hermes.

practised baptism and were faithful to the religion into which they had been born. In this case they would probably have been of the priestly clan which today still provides the intelligentsia. Such men, probably not priests but *yalufia* (literates), would be well-read in the sacred literature, and possibly might have helped their fathers to copy the manuscripts. The Hermetic writings have so much which corresponds closely to religious conceptions familiar to them in Naṣoraean gnosis that they would readily have identified the Hermes of the *Poimandres* as their own Manda-ḏ-Hiia or Mara-ḏ-Rabutha. Such passages as that in *Poimandres*, which speak of the bisexual *νοῦς*, 'éxistant comme vie et lumière' in the translation of Festugière and Nock,[1] would be easily recognized by them as the mystical Palm-tree and Wellspring, or perhaps as the bisexual Adam who was both of these according to the secret teaching.

It is hardly to be wondered at if Harranian Ṣābians gave names such as 'Hermes' or 'Agathodaemon'[2] to Moslem inquirers, instead of sacred names which were never to be uttered in the presence of unbelievers.

Some Harranian Ṣābians appear to have truly been pagans and the term 'Ṣābian', as Chwolsohn showed, was applied later indiscriminately to any non-Moslem, non-Jew, or non-Christian, in the easy, inexact fashion of those who despised such religions and thought them unworthy of serious consideration. In the *Fihrist* (see Chwolsohn, op. cit., p. 18) we are told that in Harran there was intermarriage

[1] 'Or le Noûs Dieu, étant mâle et femelle, existant comme vie et lumière, enfanta d'une parole un second Noûs démiurge qui, étant dieu du feu et du souffle, façonna des Gouverneurs, sept en nombre, lesquels enveloppent dans leurs cercles le monde sensible; et leur gouvernement se nomme la Destinée' (A. D. Nock and A. J. Festugière, *Hermès Trismégiste* (Paris, 1945), vol. i, Traité, I. ix).

[2] There is no mention of Hermes or Agathodaemon in Mandaean books. The Harranians seem to have quoted Hermes and 'Ārāni' as founders of their religion! They probably referred to Seth and Enoš (Šitil and Anuš in Mandaic), for Shahrastānī identified Agathodaemon with the former and Hermes with the latter. Al-Qifti calls Agathodaemon the 'teacher' of Hermes. Seth or Setheus figures in the Coptic gnostic texts. The Sethians were attacked by Christian heresiologists (e.g. Hippolytus in his *Refutation of all Heresies*, bk. x, chap. vii).

According to M. Jean Doresse's survey of the Khenoboskion gnostic books (*Les Livres secrets des gnostiques d'Égypte*) a number of the manuscripts found there belong to the Sethian group. In *Koptisch-Gnostische Schriften*, Vol. 1 (see p. xii, n. 1) 'Setheus' figures in several obscure passages, e.g. as 'lord of the Pleroma' (363: 32), 'crowned demiurge' (350: 7), &c. Hermes (op. cit. 234: 30 f.) is said by 'Jesus' to be the third great archon.

For the Mandaean Seth and Anuš see above, Chapter IV.

between false and genuine Ṣābians, which implies that a number of both were living in that city.

Let us consider the names of some Harranian Ṣābians who became famous under the Abbasids as scholars, physicians, and so on. We find the name Abu'l-Fatḥ-*al-Mandāi* (i.e. 'the Mandaean'), and Ibrāhīm-ibn-*Zahrūn*-ibn-Ḥabbūn-al-Ḥarrānī, whose son was another *Zahrūn*, and Hilāl-ibn-Ibrāhīm-ibn-*Zahrūn*-abu'l-Huṣain-al-Ṣābi-al-Ḥarrānī. To this very day 'Zahrūn' is the name most favoured by Mandaeans: I know many so called and it is a name reserved for them. Other names favoured by them are Šitil (Seth), Anuš (Enos), and Hirmis or Hirmiz (Hermes or Ohrmazd?[1]), although the last is a 'worldly' name, not a *malwaša* (baptismal name).

It is hardly surprising that the name 'Hirmiz' (which by Assyrians is used in the form 'Hormuz' and 'Hormuzd'[2]) on account of its Magian connexion should be shunned as a religious name. It never appears in colophons. The Mandaeans were settled round the Tigris, Euphrates, and Karun rivers, with headquarters at Ṭīb. Their neighbours before the arrival of the Moslems were Magians, and although we find Persian names such as 'Shahpūr' in colophons, the name 'Hirmiz' could not, on grounds of orthodoxy, be used for baptism.[3]

For a similar reason, perhaps, no prayer or hymn in the Mandaean liturgy is addressed to Fire, although a fire is essential for every Mandaean rite, including baptism. Its purity is carefully preserved, fuel receives triple immersion, incense is cast into it, and the sacred bread baked on it. Moreover, in *ATŠ* it is said that 'Without fire no baptism can ascend to the House of Life.' To exalt it unduly, however, might have been unwise: fire-temples and Magian priests were close at hand.[4]

[1] Although the work of several authors, the Hermetic writings shelter under the name of Hermes. Greek syncretists, because the Egyptian god Thoth was the scribe of the gods, found his equivalent in their own god Hermes, that aerial immortal who conducted departed spirits to the next world and spoke to mortals in dreams. This fictitious Hermes: could he have been a syncretistic corruption of the Pehlevi Ohrmuzd, the deified principle of good, the Zoroastrian Ahura-Mazda? If so, it was by route of Jewish-Alexandrian gnosticism in close touch with Galilaean and Samaritan circles.

[2] The monastery of Rabban Hormuzd is a much-visited shrine.

[3] Yet the Mandaean genius of baptism is the Persian Bihram (see p. 65)! I suggest that he became attached to the baptism-cult before the settlement in southern Persia and Mesopotamia, when Jewish gnostics were in close touch with Magian mystics in the first century, in the West.

[4] Cf. the omission of fire in the list of witnesses necessary at an Elkasaite immersion, which, according to Hippolytus, were sky, water, holy spirits, the angel of prayer, oil, salt, and earth. According to Epiphanius (Haer. xix. 1) 'Elxai' ordered honour to be paid to 'salt, water, earth, bread, sky, ether, and wind'.

MANDAEAN SOURCES

A. *Unpublished Manuscripts Quoted*

Alma Rišaia Rba, Bodleian Library MS. *DC* 41. (An illustrated, secret initiation text.)

Alma Rišaia Zuṭa, Bodleian Library MS. *DC* 48. (Illustrated.)

Diwan ḏ-Nahrwata, Bodleian Library MS. *DC* 7. (Illustrated.)

Diwan Malkuta 'laita, Bodleian Library MS. *DC* 34. (An illustrated, secret initiation text.)

Ginza Rba, Sidra Rba ḏ-Mara ḏ-Rabuta, Sidra ḏ-Adam, Bodleian Library MS. *DC* 22. (This contains parts omitted in Petermann's transliterated Ginza (*Thesaurus Liber*, &c.), see below.)

Šarḥ ḏ-Maṣbuta-Rabtia, Bodleian Library MS. *DC* 50.

Šarḥ ḏ-Parwanaiia, Bodleian Library MS. *DC* 24.

Šarḥ ḏ-Ṭabahata, Bodleian Library MS. *DC* 42.

Šarḥ ḏ-Taraṣa ḏ-taga ḏ-Šišlam-Rba, British Museum MS. Or. 6592. (A secret text.)

Šarḥ ḏ-Zihrun-Raza-Kasia, Bodleian Library MS. *DC* 27.

B. *Published Manuscripts*

Alf Trisar Šuialia: A Thousand and Twelve Questions. Text, with transliteration and translation by E. S. Drower (Institut für Orientforschung, Deutsche Akademie der Wissenschaften, Berlin, 1960).

The Book of the Zodiac (*Sfar Malwašia*). Text and translation by E. S. Drower (The Royal Asiatic Society, 1949).

The Canonical Prayerbook of the Mandaeans. Text in facsimile and translation by E. S. Drower (E. J. Brill, Leiden, Holland, 1959).

Codex Nasareus, Liber Adami Appellatus. Syriac text and Latin translation by M. Norberg (Lund, 1815–16, 3 vols.).

Das Johannesbuch der Mandäer. Text and translation by M. Lidzbarski (Töpelmann, Giessen, 1915, 2 vols.).

Diwan Abathur. Text and translation by E. S. Drower in *Studi e Testi*, 151 (Biblioteca Apostolica Vaticana, Rome, 1950).

Ginzā: der Schatz oder das große Buch der Mandäer. Translated by M. Lidzbarski (Vandenhoeck u. Ruprecht, Göttingen, 1925).

Haran Gawaita and *Maṣbuta ḏ-Hibil-Ziwa*. Text in facsimile and translation by E. S. Drower in *Studi e Testi*, 176 (Biblioteca Apostolica Vaticana, Rome, 1953).

Mandäische Liturgien. Translated by M. Lidzbarski (Sitzungsberichte der Preussischen Akademie, Phil.-hist, Kl., Bd. 17, no. 1, Berlin, 1920).

Šarḥ ḏ-Qabin ḏ-Šišlam-Rba. Transliterated and translated by E. S. Drower, Biblica et Orientalia no. 12 (Pontificio Istituto Biblico, Rome, 1950).

Thesaurus Liber Magnus vulgo 'Liber Adami' appellatus, opus Mandaeorum summi ponderis. Descripsit et edidit, H. Petermann (Weigel, Leipzig, 1867, 2 vols.).

For Mandaean rites, customs, &c., see E. S. Drower, *The Mandaeans of Iraq and Iran* (Clarendon Press, Oxford, 1937), and *Water into Wine* (John Murray, 1956). References to other non-Mandaic sources will be found in the footnotes.

INDEX

Abad-ukšar, 65.
Abathur (*Abatur*), 29, 34 f., 42, 64 f., 77; A. of the Scales, 64, 67 n. 3, 79; Diwan A., xiii.
Adakas, 32, 35 ff.; A. Mana, A. Ziwa, 35, 37 f., 102 f., 105.
Adam, cosmic, 5 *passim*; A. *qadmaia*, Qadmon or Kadmon, *see* Chap. III; A. Kasia (the mystic or secret Adam), xi, xv, 12 n. 2, 18 f., 21–33, 37, 40, 43, 60, 70 *et passim*; Body of A. Kasia, 74–80, 104; vast size of A., 26 n. 3, 93; sons of A., 34–38; *A. Pagria* (Physical Adam), 103; A.-Shaq, 30 f.; *A. Shaq-Ziwa*, 72, 75 n. 2; Adam Alkasai, 92; as Christ, 96; Book of A., 97; A. son of El, 101; A. as king-priest, 101 n. 2, 104; Last A., 102.
Adonai, 102 and n. 1.
Agathodaemon, 111, 112 n. 2.
Ahaba ḏ-mania (Giving of clothes), 51, 70, 74, 109. *See* Clothes, *Rasta*, Vestments.
Ahura Mazda, Ohrmazd, 41, 61, 67 n. 2, 113.
'*Aina*, *see* Wellspring.
Āl-Haṣiḥ, 92, 93 n. 1.
Alexandrian schools, 91, 99; *see also* Jews, Alexandrian.
Alphabet, ABG, 17–20, 26.
Anahita, 104 and n. 1.
Anana, 36 n. 1; *A.-Ziwa*, 26.
Anatan, 57 f.
Andreas, Prof. F., 64.
Anuš, 36 n. 3, 37 f., 64; (Enos= *Anuš*), 82, 85, 111 f., 112 n. 2; Anuš-'uthra, 39.
Apuleius, 57.
Archetype(s), *see* Counterparts, Fravahr; world of, 44 f.; in Clementines, 46; archetype of priest and bridegroom, 60.
Aristobulus, 81, 99.
Aristotle, 83.
Artabanus, xiii.
Ašganda (pl. *ašgandia*), 57, 73, 75, 108 f.
Augustine, St., 82 n. 3, 92.
Avesta, 40.
Ayar (ether, air), 14 ff.; *see also* Ether; *A.-Dakia* (pure ether), personified, 71, 75; *A.-Ziwa*, 14 f.; *A.-Rba*, 14 f., 75, 77.

Ba and *bai*, xv, 8, 32.
Babylon, Babylonia, x f., 100; exodus into, 104.
Banner(s), 57, 61 f., 65, 67.
Baptism, 24 n. 3, 65 *et passim*; of Adam, 31; Great B. (360 baptisms), 56 f., 68 n. 2, 70; b. of children, 68 and n. 3; baptismal sacraments, 79, 93.
Benveniste, Prof. E., 65.
Bihram, 19, 65 f., 67 n. 2.
Bimanda, *bit-manda*, xii n. 4, 33; *see also* Cult-hut.
Birth, of spiritual body, 78, and n. 2.
Blood, Adam's, 30; b.-sacrifice, *see* Sacrifice.
Body (*ṣṭuna*), xvii, 13; *see also* '*ṣṭuna*; conception and birth of spiritual b., 74–80, 98; b. of Adam, xvii, 27 f., 104.
Bones, 29 n. 5, 42.
Bousset, Dr. W., 46.
Boyce, Dr. Mary, 21 n. 1, 42 n. 5.
Brandt, A. J. H. Wilhelm, 14 n. 3, 64 and n. 5, 68 n. 3, 93 n. 1, 95 n. 3.
Bread, 3 n. 1; sacramental, 42, 51, 67; *see also pihta*, *faṭira*; baking b., 62 n. 1, 67; B. of Life, 86.
Bultmann, Prof. D. R., 86 n. 4, 88 n. 1.
Bundahišn, 22 n. 1, 28 n. 1.
Burial, 29 n. 5, 48.
Burkitt, Prof. E. C., 95 n. 3.

Canaan, 93 n. 1, 101.
Carmel, 84 f.
Celibacy, 73, 97.
Cerdo, 91.

Christ (= Messiah, or Anointed One), 88 n. 2, 94 f.; Elkasaite C., 96; Sampsaean C., 96.
Chwolsohn, Dr. D., 92 n. 2, 98 n. 1, 111 f.
Circumcision, 98, 102 f.
Clementines, 45 and n. 1, 46, 77, 88, 93 n. 1.
Clothes, at death, 73; *see also Rasta, Ahaba-ḏ-mania.*
Column of glory, *see 'ṣṭun.*
Commemoration (*dukrana*), 74; c. prayer, 87 n. 3, 98, 101, 110.
Communion (*laufa*), *see Laufa.*
Coronation, 61.
Counterpart(s) (*dmut, dmuta,* pl. *dmauata*), 38, 39–46, 54 f.; world of, *see Mšunia Kušṭa.*
Creation, 1 ff., 13, 18 f., 24 ff.; of Adam, 35; unsuccessful, 34, 48.
Creator, Jewish, 88 n. 2, 89.
Crown, 6, 20 n. 3, 26, 44, 60 f., 80; consecration of Adam's c., 71; crowning, 104; *see also* Coronation.
Cullmann, O., 88 n. 1.
Cult-hut, xii n. 4, 31; *see also Škinta.*

Dabahata (*ṭabahata*), the *masiqta,* so-called, 43, 71.
Darkness, 5; world(s) of, 58; *see also* Underworld; Well of D., 36; King of D., 56; warriors of, 57.
Dates (*sindirka*), 31 n. 3, 69 f.; *see also* Palm-tree.
Davies, the Rev. W. D., D.D., 32, 102 n. 2.
Death, 50 f.; ritual meals at and after d., 68, 70, 73; d.-rites, 73; *see also* Letter.
Demiurge, 5, 25 n. 1, 88, 98, 112 n. 1.
Demons (disease- and lunacy-d.s), 68 n. 1, 94 n. 1.
Denkart, 46 n. 1.
Diaspora, xi, 82, 99.
Dmut, dmuta, see Counterpart; *Dmuthiia,* 43 f.
Docetic heresy, 96 n. 1.
Dodd, Prof. C. H., 86 n. 4.
Dog, mad, 94.
Doresse, Dr. J., xii n. 1, 25 n. 1, 112 n. 2.
Dositheus, 91, 100.
Dove, 8, 30 nn. 2 and 4, 32, 71, 75, 79.
Driver, Prof. G. R., C.B.E., 82 n. 2, 93 n. 1.
Drop(s), 13; the D. (*Niṭufta*), 59.
Dualism, 45; *see also* Counterparts.
Dukrana, see Commemoration.

Ebionites, 45 n. 1, 67 n. 1, 95 and n. 1, 96 f.
Egg, of Life, 14; of soul and silk-worm, 51 f.
Egypt, x, xv; *masiqta* for Egyptians, xv n. 2.
El (עיל), 75 n. 2, 93 n. 1, 98 and n. 1, 102; 'El- or Āl-, Kasai, 101.
Elchasai (Elkasai, Elxai, &c.), 14 n. 3, 26 n. 3, 46, 93, 97, 102 f.; Elkasaites, 73 n. 1, 92 ff.; their book, 93, 97; Elxai, 113 n. 4.
Eleazar ben Yehudah, 44 f.
Ennoia, 81, 89.
Enoch, Book of, 81 f.
Enos (*Anuš*), 81.
Epiphanius, xiv and n. 3, 14 n. 3, 73 n. 3, 92, 94 ff., 97, 98 n. 1, 101 f., 105 n. 2, 113 n. 4.
Essenes, 14, 32, 94 f., 97, 98.
Ether (*Ayar*), 14 ff., 24 f., 44, 48, 52, 55, 77; world of e., 49, 86, 90 n. 4.
Eusebius, 89, 91, 95.
Eve (Hawa), 23, 34 f., 37, 42, 82 and n. 2, *et passim.*

Fars, 62.
Father, the, 6, 9, 12 ff., 24, 27, 48, 53, 59, 67, 70 f., 75 f., 78, 83 *et passim*; Father and Mother, the androgynous figure of, 92.
Faṭiria (sing. *faṭira*), 75 n. 5, 60 f., 76 *et passim.*
Festugière, the Rev. Fr. A. J., O.P., 22 n. 1, 37 n. 2, 112 and n. 1.
Fihrist, al-, ix, 112.
Fire, fire-altar, 61 f., 62 n. 1, 67, 87, 113; kinds of f., 90 n. 1; unbegotten, 90.
Fish, 70 f., 86.
Fravahr (*fravaši*), 40 f.
Fravardin Yašt, 41.

Gaf, 29, 58.
Galilee, xi, xv, 98, 100 f.
Ganzibra (pl. *ganzibria*), head-priest in Mandaean Church, 57, 73 *et passim*.
Gaster, Dr. Moses, xv.
Gaster, Theodore, 92 n. 1.
Gayomard (= Kayomart, Gayomart), 103; *see also* Kayomart.
Gematria, 83.
Gershevitch, I., 65 n. 1.
Ghirshmann, Dr. R., 99 f.
Girdle, sacred, 71.
Gnostic idiom, 55, 82 ff.; (Coptic) gnostic texts, xii, 112 n. 2; *see also* Khenoboskion.
Grave, 29 n. 5.
Greek influence, xi, 99 ff., 100 n. 1.

Habšaba, *see* Sunday.
Hag and Mag, 19.
Hair, cut or uncut, 95 nn. 2 and 3, 108.
Halalta (rinsing-water, water for washing), 76.
Hamar-kana, 86; *hamra*, *see* Wine.
Haoma, 31 n. 3.
Haran Gawaita, xi, xiii, xv, 37, 104, 105 n. 2.
Harran, xiii f., 37, 104 f., 112; Harranian Ṣabians, 112 ff.
Hasidim, 44.
Hawa (Eve), *see* Eve; *Hawa Kasia*, 36, 40, 43, 97.
Hegesippus, 95 n. 2.
Henning, Prof., 61.
Hermes and Hermetica, 22 n. 1, 37 n. 2, 45, 99, 111 n. 1, 112 and n. 2, 113 n. 1; modern name Hermes, 113.
Hibil, 36, 38.
Hibil-Ziwa, 6, 19, 29, 36, 42, 51, 56–59, 63, 97.
Hieronymus, 95 n. 2, 96 n. 3.
Hippocrates, 28 n. 1.
Hippolytus, 2 n. 1, 19 n. 6, 26 n. 3, 89 f., 90 n. 4, 92 f., 94, 113 n. 4.
Ḥokhmah and Binah, 90 n. 2.
Hooke, Prof. S. H., 75 n. 2.
Hormuzd, Rabban, 113 n. 2.
Hyginus, 91.

Incense, 67.
Inhalation rites, 87.
Irenaeus, 2 n. 1, 25 n. 1, 26 n. 3, 37 n. 2, 67 n. 1.

James the Just, 90 n. 3, 95 n. 2.
Jerome, *see* Hieronymus.
Jerusalem, xi, 27 n. 2, 37, 39, 98; destruction of, xi.
Jesus, xi f., 39, 46, 61 n. 1, 82 f., 84 n. 2, 89, 91 f., 95 nn. 2 and 3, 96, 102, 103 n. 1, 112 n. 2.
Jews, xi, 39; Babylonian, 99; Greek, 100; Alexandrian, 81 f., 113 n. 1; Jewish mystics, 44 f., *see also* Kabbalism; Naṣoraean hatred of Jews, 98; Influence of Jews on Iran and vice versa, 100, 103 ff.; Jewish Creator, 88 n. 2; Jewish Christians, 67 n. 1, 88, 94 f., 102 f.; *see also* Ebionites.
John Apokryphon, 27 n. 1.
John the Baptist, xi, xiv, 37, 46, 65, 89, 91, 101.
Jonas, Dr. Hans, 100 n. 1.
Jordan, xiv, 13 f., 18, 23 f., 37, 41, 93 *et passim*; Jordan-baptism, xiv n. 2; Jordan-valley, xi.
Josephus, 14 n. 3, 98 n. 1.
Judaea, xi, 98, 100 f.; Judaeo-Christians, *see* Jews and Ebionites.
Judgement, Day of, 86, 97.

Kabbalism, 21 n. 2, 44.
Kaiumart and Kayomartaeans, 103.
Kali, 13.
Kelly, Dr. J. N. D., 96 n. 1.
Khenoboskion papyri (Nag-Hammadi MSS.), xii n. 1, 25 n. 1, 36, 112 n. 2.
Kimṣa, 31.
Kindi, al-, 111.
King(s), kingliness (*malka*, pl. *malkia*; *malkuta*), 24 n. 1; *see also* Priests; 'Uthras, 56 ff.
Kušṭa, K. rites, 24 n. 2, 37, 39 n. 1, 55, 108; K. personified, 65; sister in K., 43, 47; *see also* Mšunia Kušṭa.

Lake, Prof. Kirsopp, D.D., 91 n. 3.
Lamb, slaughter of, 32 n. 1; Paschal, 61 n. 1.

Laufa or *lofani* (union, communion), 43 n. 1, 51, 67 f., 106.
Left, *see* Right and L., and Women and L.
Legge, F., 83.
Letter (the sacrament so-named), 26 and n. 1, 42 f., 50, 57, 59, 73 f., 109.
Letters of the alphabet, 17, 29 n. 1; *see also* Alphabet.
Lidzbarski, Prof. Mark, xiv n. 3, 7 f., 31 n. 2, 35 n. 5, 37 n. 2.
Life, *passim*; the Great L., 1 ff., 3 n. 1; the (Great) First L., 4, 85, 97; the Second ditto, 4; the Third ditto, 4; the Sign of, 5; House of, 35 f., 54, 62 n. 1; Family of, 86.
Light (*Ziwa* = active, creative, male, cosmic, *see Ziwa* and *Yawar*), 1 ff.; (*Nhura*, female aspect of, 6); L. and darkness, 5, 53, 86; King of L., 3, 56 *et passim*.

Macrocosm and microcosm, 22 n. 1, 25, 28 n. 2, 35, 82 *et passim*; *see also* Adam.
Macuch, Dr. Rudolf, xiv.
Magian(s), 12, 45, 87, 100, 103, 113; Simon the M., 90; *see also* Simon.
Male and Female, 23 ff.; male organ, 28 f.
Mambuga (or *mambuha*), 37, 42 f., 93.
Man, the Heavenly, 97 f., 104, *see also* Adam Kasia; Son of M., 98, 101 n. 1; Primordial M., 71 n. 7, 103 f.; *see also* Adam.
Mana (Mind), 1 f., 2 n. 1, 3, 23, 25, 35 f., 46, 47 f.; *mana*(s), 48, 50, 55, 57, 59, 80; Adakas M., *see* Adakas.
Manda-ḏ-Hiia, 48, 59, 63, 65, 85, 112; Yuzaṭaq M.-d-H., 79.
Mandaean(s), ix, xii ff., 6, 92 n. 2, 93 f., 97 *et passim*; separate from Naṣoraeans, xii n. 3, 104 f.; Mandaeans and pollution, 108 ff.
Mandelta, 109.
Manichaean(s), 21 n. 1, 83; hymns, xiii, 42 n. 5.
Mani's father, xiii.
Mara-ḏ-Rabutha, 9, 12, 18, 26 f., 39, 43, 63 f., 80 and n. 1, 112.
Marcion, 88 n. 2.
Marcus, 91.
Marriage, sacred, cosmic, 11, 20, 52 n. 1; M. of Šišlam, 60, 69; baptism before and after m., 68; Blessed Oblation at, 69 f.; early m., 73 and n. 1, 97; m. of non-virgin women, 73 n. 1.
Masiqta, xi, xv, 22, 29, 32 f., 50, 52, 55, 69, 74–80, 108; of Hibil, 31; of Zihrun-Raza-Kasia, 94; Great M., 31 n. 1; re-creation of Adakas-Ziwa at m., 105.
Mass, Orthodox, 78 n. 2.
Maṭarta (pl. *maṭarata*), 30, 35 n. 2, 50 f.
Media, xi, xiii, 100, 104 f.; *see also* Parthia.
Menander, 91, 100.
Merkelbach, Reinhold, 82 n. 3.
Messiah, xi, 92, 101, 106; Sampsaean M., 96; hour of the M., 100; *see also* Christ.
Mind, *see Mana*, *Nous*.
Miriai, 37, 43.
Mirror, 44; m. *mrara* and *gimra*, 57 f.
Miša, 106; *see also* Oil.
Mother, the, 6, 10, 12 ff., 22 n. 1, 37 n. 2, 48, 69, 71, 74 ff., 78 and n. 2.
Mšunia-Kušṭa, 35, 39–46, 53 f., 85 n. 1.
Mughtasilah, ix, xiii, 92.
Myrtle, 42, 87 and n. 2; myrtle-wreath, 6, 44, 60, 79, 104, 106.
Mysteries, 65–80.

Naaseni, the, 26 n. 3.
Nabaṭaea, Nabaṭaeans, 62, 95, 105 n. 2.
Nadīm, al- (Muhammad ben Iš'āq), ix, xiii, 92.
Nanai, Nanaia, 104.
Nasaraeans, 95 ff.; *see also* Naṣoraeans, &c.
Naṣirutha, ix ff., 12, 16, 20, 23, 26 *et passim*.
Naṣoraeans, ix, xiv, 66; (Nazoraeans, Nasoraeans), lx, 95 ff.; Mandaean-

Naṣoraeans, 98 ff.; Naṣoraean gnosis, xv f.
Nazarenes, 95 and n. 3, 96 n. 3.
Nazareth ('of N.' not 'Nazarene'), 95 n. 3.
Nazarites, 95 n. 3.
Nbaṭ-Ziwa, 63; *Nbaṭ-Hiia*, 65.
Neo-Platonism, 44 f., 46, 111.
Noah, 83, 111.
Nock, A. D., 45 n. 1, 89 n. 1, 104 n. 1, 112 and n. 1.
North, facing, 73.
Νοῦς, 5, 46, 112; *see also Mana.*
Nṣab-Hiia, 65.
Nuts (fruit and grain), 30, 29 n. 5, 32 f., 42 and n. 4.
Nyberg, Prof., 2 n. 1.

Oblation, the Blessed (*Zidqa brika*), x, 32, 37, 56 f., 59, 69–72, 93 n. 2; foods for the, 70 f., 74 f.
Ohrmazd, *see* Ahura-Mazda.
Oil (as unction for the dying, *see* Letter), 104; O. (*misa* q.v.) for the *masiqta*, 7, 31, 76 n. 1, 79.
Ophites, 25 n. 1.
Origen, 82 n. 3.
Ossaeans (Essenes?), 95, 97.

Pairs and opposites, 83; *see also* Syzygies, Counterparts.
Palm-tree, Date-palm (*sindirka*), 7 ff., 10 f., 18, 24, 27, 60, 69 n. 2, 70, 83, 112.
Pandama (the face-veil), 71.
Paragna, 31.
Parsi(s), 8, 40 and n. 1; P. regulations for purity, 108; *see also Paragna, Haoma.*
Parṣufa, 1, 3.
Parthia, xi f., 2 n. 1, 62, 93, 99; Parthian(s), 103 f.; P. hymns, 42 n. 5; P. Jews, xi, 98; influence of P. on Judaism, 100; Parthians not Zoroastrians, 100.
Parwanaiia (*Panja*), 32, 51, 109.
Passover (seder meal), 69 n. 2.
Paul, St., 32, 74, 102, 103 n. 1; Paulines, 95.
Pearl, the, soul as a, 49, 55, 58.
'Perfect', the, 43 n. 2, 73.
Persis, 62.
Personifications, 81 ff.
Peter, St., 45 n. 1, 46, 68 n. 1, 88 ff.

Phaedo, 41 n. 2.
Philo, 81 f., 99.
Pihta, 3 n. 1, 37, 42 f., 79, 93, 106.
Pillar (or Column) of Glory, 21 n. 1, 84; *see also 'ṣṭun.*
Planets, xvi, 47.
Plato, x, 41, 83 n. 1.
Poimandres, 37 n. 2, 112.
Pollution, immersion and baptism to purify, and *masiqta* a cure for, 68 n. 2, 107 f.
Priests, polluted, 66, 107; regalia of, 61; extinction of, 108; priest-king, 101 n. 2, 102, 104, 106; Priesthood, archetype of, *see* Šišlam; *see also* King(s).
Prounikos, 37 n. 2.
Ptaḥ, xv, 37 n. 2.
Ptahil, xv, 6, 35, 37 n. 2, 52, 59, 64.
Puech, H. C., 83 n. 1.
Purgatories, *see Maṭarta.*
Pythagorean influence, 45; system, 83 and n. 1.

Qifti, al-, 112 n. 2.
Qin, 6, 57 f.
Qnasa, 30 n. 3, 31, 75.
Quispel, Prof. G., xii, 9 n. 1, 23 n. 1, 27 n. 1.
Qumran, 82 n. 1, 84 n. 5, 88 n. 1, 92 n. 1.

Radiance (*Ziwa*), *see Ziwa.*
'Raising' or ascension rites, 52 n. 3, 57; *see also* Resurrection, *Masiqta.*
Ram and Rud (Height and River), 83.
Ras Shamra, 98.
Rasta (the ritual dress), 51, 71, 74, 80, 94, 109.
Rbai, the, and *rbuta*, 64.
Red or Reed Sea (*yama ḏ-Suf*), xv n. 2, 48, 83.
Reitzenstein, R., 2 n. 1, 37 n. 2, 68 n. 3.
Resurrection, body at, 29 n. 5, 30, 36, 98, *see also Masiqta*, 'Raising'; Adam Kasia a symbol of the 'resurrection body', 98.
Right and Left, 6, 13, 19.

Rudolph, Dr. Kurt, 21 n. 2.
Ruha (personified), 12 f., 47 f., 57, 59, 73 n. 1; *ruha* (spirit), 47, 49, 53, 49; *see also* Spirit.

Ṣa, the, 69 and n. 2, 70, 72 n. 2.
Sabbath, 102.
Ṣabians (Sobai, Ṣubba), ix, xiv, 92, 93 n. 1, 103, 111, 112 ff.
Sacrifice, 32 f., 33; *see also Qnasa.*
Salt, 67, 70 f., 93 n. 2.
Samaria, xv, 98, 100 f.; Samaritan(s), xv, 89, 91, 98, 100 f.
Sampsaeans, 92, 95 ff., 97 n. 1.
Saturninus, 91.
Säve-Söderbergh, Prof. Torgny, xiii and n. 1.
Schmidt, Dr. Carl, xii n. 1, 5, 45, 112 n. 2.
Schoeps, Dr. H. J., 32, 95 n. 3.
Scholem, Prof. G., 21 n. 2, 44 f.
Schonfield, Dr. Hugh J., 21 n. 2, 98 n. 1.
Sefer Yeṣirah, 14 n 1, 17, 20.
Segelberg, Dr. E., 68 n. 3.
Semen, Cosmic, 29, 76 f.
Serae (Seres?), 93 and n. 1.
Sesame, 31 n. 3, 70 f.
Seth (Šitil), 23, 29, 34, 36, 38, 47, 62, 85, 105 n. 2, 111, 112 n. 2; *masiqta* of, 76 n. 4; Sethians, 2 n. 1, 112 n. 2.
Shahrastānī, 103, 111 f.
Sige (Silence), 90.
Silkworm, 51 f.
Simat-Hiia (Treasure-of-Life), 11 f., 63.
Simon Magus, 45 n. 1, 46, 88 n. 2, 89 ff., 92, 100 f.; Simonians, 102.
Sindirka, *see* Palm-tree and Dates.
Šišlam-Rba, 18, 20, 59, 62.
Skandola, 57.
Škinta (pl. *škinata*), 2 n. 4, 20, 63.
Smith, W. B., xiv n. 3.
Sneeze, 26, 35.
Sophia, 102 n. 1; Pistis S., 112 n. 2.
Soul(s) (= *Nišimta*, pl. *nišmata*), 6, 8, 28, 36, 40 ff., 47–55; weighing the s., 67; *see also* Weighing; Book of Souls, 4, 19, 26; Vine of souls, 86 n. 3; Song of the Soul, 2 n. 1, 73.
'Ṣtun or *'ṣtuna* (column, trunk, body), 5 n. 1, 10, 13, 21 and n. 1, 27 f., 47 f., 66; *see also* Body and Pillar.
Suf, sea of, xv n. 2, 48; *see also* Red or Reed Sea.
Šulḥan 'Arukh, 107.
Sunday (*Habšaba*), personified, 65, 93.
Symbolism, 67.
Syncretism, 99.
Syzygies, 45, 83.

Tafsir Paghra, 51.
Tan(n)a, 4, 9, 11, 18, 36, 58.
Tertullian, 29 n. 5.
Theodoret, 92.
Thomas, Psalms of, xiii.
Thoth, 111 n. 1, 113 n. 1.
Ṭib, al-, xiii f., 62, 105 n. 2, 113.
Torrey, Dr., 95 n. 3.
Treasure-of-Life, *see Simat-Hiia.*
Tree of Life, 8, 90.

Underworld, a part of the Cosmic Body, 27 ff.
Union, the Sacred, *see* Marriage; communion, *see Laufa*; mystic, ultimate u., 53 f., 55.
'Ur, 57, 59.
'Uthras, 2 n. 3, 4, 8, 15 n. 2, 24, 56 *et passim.*

Valentinus, 25 n. 1, 91; Valentinians, 2 n. 1, 102 n. 1.
Van Buren, Mrs., 8 n. 2.
Vay or Vayu, 15, 90 n. 4.
Vegetarianism, 95 n. 2, 102.
Verethragna, 65.
Vestments, *see Rasta.*
Vine, 84 and nn. 1 and 2, 85 f.
Virgin Birth, 94.

Waerden, B. L. van der, 83 n. 1.
Waitz, Hans, 45 n. 1.
Water as baptismal sacrament, 67 n. 1; Living, or turbid or stagnant, 6, 86; W. of life, 16, 28; W. and earth, 83 *et passim*; Waters, 1, 4; the Black waters, 58; Water into wine, *see* Wine.
Weighing souls, 64 f., 67; *see also* Abathur.

Wellspring (*'Aina*), 7 ff., 10 f., 12, 16, 18 f., 23 ff., 27, 60, 83, 112.
Widengren, Prof. Geo., 8, 21 n. 1, 75 n. 2, 101 n. 2.
Wine (*hamra*), 69 f., 86 f.; w.-cup, 69, 86; water into w., 74, 79 f., 86, 91 n. 1.
Wisdom, personified, 81, 88; W. of Solomon, 81.
Witnesses, 90 n. 4, 93 f.; to vows and oaths, 93 n. 2, 113 n. 4.
Womb, the Cosmic, 28 f., 51, 69, 74, 86 n. 2.
Women, 73 n. 1.
Word, the, *Mimra*, logos, &c., 3, 17, 80; Mahzian the W., 26, 75.
Wreath, *see* Crown, Myrtle-w.

Yahia, *see* John; *Drašia ḏ-Y.*, 101 n. 1.
Yahweh, 99.
Yaldabaoth, 25 n. 1, 37 n. 2.
Yama ḏ-Suf, *see* Suf, and Red or Reed Sea.
Yaqūt, the geographer, 62, 105 n. 2.
Yawar, *Yawar-Ziwa*, 1 ff., 5 ff., 11, 15, 23, 35, 48, 63, 77; as Vine, 84.
Yazidis, 32.
Yexai, 97.
Yušamin, 60.

Zaehner, Prof. R. C., 12, 22 n. 1, 28 n. 1, 46 n. 1, 77 n. 3, 90 n. 6.
Zahriel, 19, 58 f.
Zahrun, name, 113.
Zidqa brika, 93 n. 2; *see also* Oblation, Blessed.
Zihrun, see *Masiqta*.
Ziwa, 1, 15 *et passim*; Hibil-Z., *see* Hibil; Adakas-Z., *see* Adakas; Ayar-Z., 14; Yawar-Z., *see* Yawar; Nbaṭ-Z., 63.
'zlat, 11, 12, 20, 60.
Zodiac, 83; Book of the Z., 98 n. 1.
Zoroaster, Zoroastrians, 12 n. 1, 29 n. 5.
Zurvan, 22 n. 1, 28 n. 1, 46 n. 1, 90 n. 4.

www.ingramcontent.com/pod-product-compliance
Lightning Source LLC
Chambersburg PA
CBHW070919160426
43193CB00011B/1518
* 9 7 8 1 5 3 2 6 9 7 6 3 0 *